The Simple Art of
RIBBON DESIGN

The Simple Art of
RIBBON DESIGN

Deborrah
Henry

WATSON-GUPTILL
PUBLICATIONS
New York

Display photography by Pat Pollard
Step-by-step instructional photography by Deborrah Henry
The original art shown in the photograph on page 43 was painted by Rich Nichols

First published in 1999 by Watson-Guptill Publications,
a division of BPI Communications, Inc.,
1515 Broadway, New York, N.Y. 10036

Library of Congress Cataloging-in-Publication Data
Henry, Deborrah.
    The simple art of ribbon design / Deborrah Henry.
       p. cm. — (Watson-Guptill crafts)
    ISBN 0-8230-4832-2
    1. Ribbon work. 2. Ribbon flowers. I. Title. II. Series.
TT850.5.H46 1999
746'.0476—DC21   99-30217
                                            CIP

Manufactured in China

First printing, 1999

2 3 4 5 6 7 8 9 / 07 06 05 04 03 02 01 00

Senior Editor: Candace Raney
Edited by Joy Aquilino
Designed by Jay Anning
Graphic production by Hector Campbell

ACKNOWLEDGMENTS

Thanks must first be given to the many women who have made ribbon flowers, thus allowing us to add our own 21st-century flair to an art form that has been mastered and manifested over the centuries in many clever and creative ways.

I would also like to thank the women who inspired me by reintroducing a Victorian art to the present day: Kathy Risso, Katheryn Foutz, Candace Kling, and Elly Sienkiewicz.

Thanks also to my sisters, Brooke and Diana, for teaching me; and to my mother, Hanah, for creating some of the most beautiful ribbons ever.

I'm grateful to Ron, Ashley, and Cara for supporting me during the unfoldment of life and of this book.

Thanks most of all to God for making all of this happen.

Contents

Introduction   9

Ribbon Flower Supplies   10
Ribbons for Flowers   12
Soft-Edge Ribbon   12
Wire-Edge Ribbon   13
Shopping for Ribbons   14
Where to Shop   14
Making a Selection   14
Other Essential Supplies   18
Needles   18
Thread   18
Thimbles   18
Scissors   18
Glue Gun and Glue Sticks   18
Wire and Wire Cutters   18
Storage Box or Basket   19

Making Ribbon Flowers, Step by Step   20
Preparing Your Ribbons   22
Rinsing   22
Pressing   22
Basting   23
Creating with Ribbon   24
Exercise: Getting in Touch with Your Creative Energy   25
Storing Finished Projects   27

Ribbon Flower Designs   28
Posies   30
Peonies   34
Roses   38
Hollyhocks   42
Chrysanthemums   46
Pansies   50
Poppies   54
Daisies   58

Finishing Your Flowers   62

Flower Centers   64
Buttons   65
Ribbons   66
Polymer Clay   69
Stems   70
Leaves   72
Easy Leaves   72
Folded Leaves   73
Scalloped Leaves   76
Wired Leaves   77

Wearables and Accessories   78

Ribbon Flower Corsages   80
Simple Rose Corsage   80
Corsage Bouquet   81
"Blooming" Hat   83
Basket of Flowers Tote   85
Pansy Pouch   86

Gifts and Special Occasions   90

Gift Tie-Ons   92
Tussie-Mussies   94
Holiday Stockings   96
Holiday Ornaments   98
Wreaths   100

The Beribboned Table   102

Centerpieces   104
Napkin Rings or Ties   106
Picture Frame Placecards   107
Streamer Bouquets   108

Source Directory   110
Index   111

Introduction

My mother, Hanah, was the artist in the family when I was growing up. In addition to creating beautiful garments, sculpture, and other forms of art, she would decorate a special table to express the sentiment of each holiday or season. Whether she had made a scary witch for Halloween or a miniature tree replete with tiny ornaments for Christmas, she communicated to us that something warm and wonderful was coming. I carried on the tradition of making something to mark the passing of a special event or holiday, so that today my children remind me to bring out the decorations that help them recall the warmth they felt when they were very young as each season and holiday drew near.

In the late 1980s, my mother took the creative lead once again by deciding to "find her feminine side" (as she put it) by dyeing silk, and began experimenting with silk cut into ribbon widths. My mother is a master colorist as well as an artist and inventor, so she became serious about learning to dye rolls of ribbon consistently in the most beautiful colors I had ever seen. It wasn't long before she created "Hanah Silk," a line of hand-dyed silk ribbons in a wide range of colors and widths. Because she didn't want to manufacture the ribbon single-handedly, my mother drafted my sister Brooke, who as an experienced crafter was the logical choice for a partner. My other sister, Diana, and I simply could not avoid the allure of the family venture, and left our respective careers (mine as a psychotherapist, hers as a teacher) to join the "ribbon revolution."

We began attending wholesale trade shows in order to sell the ribbon. At our very first show we hung yards and yards of ribbons all over the booth. The attendees were intrigued and attracted by the exquisite colors and textures, but had no idea how the ribbons could be used in crafts. As a creative person I was surprised that people wouldn't know what to do with the ribbons, but I realized that I had to devise applications for them in order to increase their marketability. Making flowers with wire-edge ribbon was a popular craft at the time, so I began experimenting by making flowers with our soft-edge ribbons. I was pleasantly surprised that my flowers were more beautiful and natural-looking than wire-edge flowers. Thus began my flower-making adventure.

I eventually began my own business, "Creative Kits," which allow people to experiment with specific lengths and colors of ribbons before buying them on their own. I now travel around the country and abroad teaching beginning crafters how to make ribbon flowers and, through those efforts, how to liberate and meet the challenges of their creativity. This approach reflects my education and experience as a psychotherapist as well as my own creative drive. I believe that the creative urge is an inherent part of human nature that, sadly, many people lose or repress as they become adults. Each of us has unique gifts that make us special and give us something important to contribute to the world. Self-expression can relax us, heal us, and occasionally bring us closer to a feminine spirit that, in many cases, has been forgotten or simply abandoned. It is my intention to teach people to create beautiful and original art by giving them simple techniques that can be used with a variety of materials, thus offering them an opportunity to express themselves without having to worry too much about how it's done.

If you are inspired by this book, I urge you to use it to learn *how* to create, then to use that knowledge and experience to bring your own ideas to fruition. To get started, all you need is a desire to create something and to know how to baste (if you don't, see page 23). On page 110 is a list of sources for the materials that are used to create the flowers shown in the book, so that you can begin your creative odyssey by reproducing them exactly. All in all, very little preparation is required for the ultimate goal: to realize your own creative potential. Have fun, and happy creating!

Ribbon Flower Supplies

Ribbons for Flowers

Crafters today can choose from an astounding variety of ribbons produced in myriad colors, prints, fabrics, textures, and widths. For the purposes of making flowers, ribbon can be divided into two basic categories: soft-edge and wire-edge. In addition, flowers can be made from fabric that has been cut *on the bias,* or at a 45-degree angle to its weave.

SOFT-EDGE RIBBON

Soft-edge ribbon has *selvedges,* or edges, that are either cut or woven. To create the flowers that are shown in this book, I used several different kinds of soft-edge ribbon, including silk, velvet, suede, and polyester. Not only is it much easier to make flower using lightweight, pliable ribbon, but the softer the fabric from which a ribbon is made, the softer the

flower. I've found that hand-dyed silk ribbon is not only extremely pliable and easy to work with, but because silk absorbs dye unlike any other textile, it duplicates the soft, natural appearance of real flowers better than any other kind of ribbon. Although polyester and other synthetic-fiber ribbons that are intended to emulate silk are the least expensive and the most widely available, they are the most difficult to manipulate, so the results are not always as desirable as when softer fabrics like silk and velvet are used. In my opinion, hand-dyed silk ribbon is without equal, mainly because I favor a softer-looking flower. Since you may prefer more variety in your "ribbon garden," experiment with several different kinds of soft-edge ribbon, then decide for yourself which are the most beautiful and easiest to handle.

Soft-edge ribbon comes in a wide range of colors and fabrics. (Right) *Several spools of beautifully hand-dyed variegated silk ribbon.* (Below) *An arrangement of organdy, velvet, and pleated ribbons.*

WIRE-EDGE RIBBON

Wire-edge ribbon is made by stitching a fine wire along a ribbon's selvedges. Many different kinds of ribbon are made with wired edges, including some beautiful French and variegated ones. Wire-edge ribbon is currently very popular among ribbon crafters because it's easy to mold into shape and in some instances doesn't require basting, whereas soft-edge ribbon always does. In fact, two of the "baste-along-the-bottom-edge" flower designs in this book—the peony (see page 34), which can also be modified to look like a rose (page 38), and the poppy (page 54)—can be made with wire-edge ribbon. Wire-edge ribbon is also a good choice for making leaves because it's easy to twist into shape. In contrast to soft-edge ribbon, and hand-dyed silk ribbon in particular, wire-edge ribbon produces flowers and leaves with a spiky, sculptured appearance.

Give wire-edge ribbon a try to see whether you enjoy working with it, and whether you like the look of the flowers and leaves it makes. Before purchasing any wire-edge ribbon, check the design instructions of the flower you have in mind to make sure it can be used.

Wire-edge ribbon can be twisted, pleated, and curved into a variety of shapes.

Shopping for Ribbons

You now have a little information about ribbons—you know what the two basic categories are—but how do you go about choosing them for a project, and where do you find them? Experimentation is the best way to sort out your creative preferences, but that approach can become time-consuming and expensive. So that you won't have to do too much sampling, I have included more than one example of each flower in order to show how different ribbons will work in a particular design. Each individual ribbon can be used to make a unique flower, and deciding which ribbons appeal to you most is part of the creative process.

WHERE TO SHOP

Once you're ready to purchase ribbons, the question of where to begin arises. Ribbons are usually sold in craft and fabric stores, and can also be found in some department stores, stationery stores, and specialty ribbon stores. If you can't find ribbons at a local retailer, or if you live in a remote area (as I do), then shopping through mail-order catalogs or the Internet may be the way to go. (See page 110 for a list of mail-order sources for ribbon, including suppliers of hand-dyed silk ribbon.) The Internet is a particularly exciting way to shop, as it allows crafters to buy from far-flung suppliers, even those in Canada and Europe. To find sites that sell high-quality silk and other soft-edge ribbons, input "French ribbons" and "specialty ribbons" into your search engine. For wire-edge ribbon, search for "craft ribbons."

No matter where or how you shop, always keep a record of where you purchased your ribbons, so that if you want to add flowers to a project you'll know where you can find them.

MAKING A SELECTION

A successful ribbon project has many ingredients, and the physical characteristics of the ribbons are arguably the most important. There are a variety of ways to choose ribbons, depending on your shopping and creating style. When I choose ribbons for flowermaking, I consider several attributes, including color, fabric, weight, pliability, and width, but my main emphasis is on color and softness. I'm attracted to ribbons that are unusual and beautiful, and look for ribbons that I think would make striking flowers or that inspire me in some other way. I usually start by buying 2 yards of each ribbon I like without knowing how I'm going to use them. Some crafters prefer to shop in a more planned way and choose ribbons to make specific flowers for a particular project. If I have a particular project in mind, I still begin with color and softness, then I look for other similar ribbons in a variety of widths to make an attractive color scheme. Here are a few points to keep in mind as you look at ribbons in a store, leaf through a catalog, or surf the Internet.

Color. When I began crafting I had no formal knowledge of color, so I tended to choose and use it intuitively. As a result, my projects sometimes had an amateurish quality that I wasn't entirely happy with. Over time I learned that there are rules, combinations, and formulas for artistic success, so now my approach is, first and foremost, to have fun with color, then to be conscious about my choices and how I apply what I know about color to my projects. That way, I can continue to indulge my preferences while I explore what works and what doesn't as I create each project.

Basically, there are two ways to organize colors: either by contrast or by harmony. An arrangement of flowers based on contrast emphasizes differences among colors, while one based on harmony accentuates their similarities. Of course, the best arrangements have elements of both principles.

A *color wheel* illustrates a variety of relationships among the colors of the spectrum and clarifies several aspects of contrast and harmony. Red, yellow, and blue are known as the *primary colors* because they can be mixed in various proportions to create every other color, but they themselves can't be created by mixing other colors. The *secondary colors,* orange, green, and violet, are made by mixing two primaries: red + yellow = orange; yellow + blue = green; and blue + red = violet. On the color wheel, each secondary color lies between its two primary "parents." Each of these triads makes a simple color arrangement that simultaneously expresses harmony (the secondary ties the two primaries together) and contrast (a range from light to dark).

Directly opposite each color on the wheel lies its *complement;* a pair of complementary colors set side by side within an arrangement creates intense and memorable contrast. It's important to point out that contrast isn't necessarily an unpleasant effect; many traditional holiday color schemes are comprised of two complements: for example, Christmas is red and green, and Easter is violet and yellow.

Color can also be described in terms of temperature. *Color temperature* is the perception of a color as warm or cool. Notice that the warmer colors—yellow, orange, and red—are on one side of the wheel, while the cooler ones—violet, blue, and green—are on the other. The most important aspect of color temperature is the effect it can have on an arrangement of flowers. Generally speaking, cool colors tend to recede and warm colors tend to advance, though this effect can be neutralized or even reversed, depending on the size of the element within the bouquet.

Let's consider another important aspect of color that can be used to create contrast and harmony: light and dark. The term *value* refers to a color's lightness or darkness relative to a scale of grays, from black at one extreme to white at the other. Every color can be assigned a value, from high (light) to medium to low (dark). When an arrangement consists of a single color repeated in a range of values, contrast and harmony exist side by side. A *tint* is a color that has been lightened with the addition of white, a *tone* is color that has been modified with the addition of gray or another color, and a *shade* is a color that has been darkened with the addition of black.

All these aspects of color—relationships between primaries and secondaries, between complements, as well as temperature and value—come into play when choosing ribbon colors. Begin by selecting a main

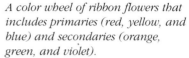

A color wheel of ribbon flowers that includes primaries (red, yellow, and blue) and secondaries (orange, green, and violet).

color, then work from there, assessing contrast and harmony as you experiment with several different combinations. Regardless of how you buy your ribbon, whether through a catalog or an Internet site or at an actual store, it's best to choose from samples of ribbon so that you can evaluate colors accurately and see firsthand how they contrast and harmonize with one another. (Each store or site will have its own specific guidelines for ordering samples.) Always maintain a sense of fun so that the process of making choices won't seem like a chore—you'll be more likely to make flowers you truly like. For guidelines on how to create an arrangement of finished flowers, see "Creating with Ribbon," page 24.

Texture. Ribbon texture is another way to add variety to a bouquet. I find that leaves look more natural when more than one green is used, especially when the ribbons are also textured in some way. I like to make my leaves with pleated and satin ribbons in a range of greens.

Another aspect of texture to consider is that of a ribbon's edges. Some of the flower designs, like the peony and the hollyhock, call for folding the ribbon in such a way that the edges are prominent in the finished flower. Ribbons with edged with picots (small ornamental loops) and frills work beautifully with these designs, as do ribbons whose edges have been dyed with another color.

Sometimes the way that the whole width of ribbon has been dyed can create a sort of visual texture. Ribbons that have been dyed with several different colors are called *variegated*. Variegated ribbons often feature a delicate blending and merging of colors, an effect that looks particularly striking in a rose, whose design requires folding the ribbon so that the center of the fold is the most prominent feature of the completed flower.

(Above) *A five-step value scale of reds, from burgundy through the palest pink.* (Right) *A bouquet pin that features tints, tones, and shades of a red-violet color.*

Width. Making a single flower design in a variety of widths is yet another way to create diversity in your ribbon "garden." In addition to considering how the ribbon's width will affect the appearance and the size of the finished flower, you need to keep in mind how it will affect the length of the ribbon you'll need to make the flower. When thinking about width, always follow this rule: The wider the ribbon, the longer it should be. Along with the instructions for each flower design, I've noted the width and length of the ribbon I used in the demonstration, which makes what I consider to be an average flower (one that fits in the palm of the hand, usually about the same size as a real flower). I've also included ranges of workable ribbon widths wherever applicable.

When experimenting with width, expect that your results will differ in appearance from the "average" flower. This isn't necessarily undesirable—that's something you have to decide for yourself, depending on your taste and the needs of your project. For example, I usually use about 1 yard of 1½-inch-wide ribbon to make an average peony (see page 34). When I use 2½-inch-wide ribbon, of which I need 1½ yards, I can make a large, floppy flower that looks similar to a magnolia. The flower isn't a peony, but it's beautiful nonetheless.

If you're unsure about what length of ribbon to use, or if a flower needs to fit into a particular space or area, you can always make the flower with the ribbon still on the spool, then cut the ribbon when the flower is the size you need.

These flowers—all pansies, yet all unique—feature ribbons in a variety of colors, textures, and widths.

Other Essential Supplies

Aside from the ribbon itself, flowermaking has very few material requirements.

Needles. When making ribbon flowers, the weight of the ribbon—the thickness of its fabric—determines which size and kind of needle is used. I basically stick to two types. For lightweight ribbons such as silk and organdy, I use milliner's needles, sizes 3 through 9, which are suitable for fine handwork and won't leave large holes in fine woven fabric. Milliner's needles will bend with frequent use, so purchase several if you plan to make many projects. For velvet and other heavyweight ribbons, I use Sharps general-purpose needles, sizes 3 through 7, which can be poked easily through a few layers of ribbons when tacking. You can find Sharps needles, which are manufactured by Coats, at most craft stores, but milliner's needles are less widely available, and may be found only at sewing stores or through mail-order sources.

Thread. Thread is an important element of making ribbon flowers because the stitching that holds the flower together must be strong and secure in order for it to last. As is the case with needles, the weight of the fabric from which the ribbon is made determines the type of thread that is used. I simplify my choices by using general-purpose thread for heavyweight ribbons and a silk-finished or quilter's cotton thread for silks and organdies. When I can't find the latter, I just use general-purpose thread for everything.

Although the stitching that's used to create the flowers isn't meant to be seen, it may be possible to catch a glimpse of it if the flowers are examined closely or if it wasn't completely hidden during the tacking process, so I recommend using the same color thread as the ribbon or fabric. Note that I used black or white thread for some of the steps in the demonstrations so that the orientation of the stitches could be seen clearly.

Thimbles. Thimbles are little metal or plastic covers for the tips of fingers, usually the thumb and forefinger, that prevents them from being poked when the needle is pushed through the ribbon. A thimble is especially handy for pushing a needle through a thick tacked "ball" at the bottom of a flower, such as when making a rose, peony, or posey.

Scissors. Since this craft involves cutting just ribbon and thread, the type of scissors you use isn't particularly significant. I use a small pair of Fiskars scissors for cutting thread, and a pair of Gingher scissors for cutting ribbon and fabric, but either could be used for both tasks.

Glue Gun and Glue Sticks. Of the two types of glue guns that are available, industrial-use and craft-use, the latter, in either a standard size or a mini version, is more appropriate for making ribbon flowers. After using a variety of glues and burning my fingers numerous times, I highly recommend that you purchase a glue gun that will accept either low- or variable- (high-low) temperature glue, both of which have good adhesion but remain relatively cool as they are dispensed. If you must use high-temperature glue, do so carefully. In some applications, as when making stems, the glue may come into contact with fingers, and hot glue can cause blisters.

Wire and Wire Cutters. The gauge of wire that is used to make a stem depends on the size and weight of the flower it will be attached to. When choosing wire for this purpose, keep in mind that paper-covered wire tends to hold glue better than plain wire. Paper-covered wire can be found at craft and floral supply stores. I use a heavyweight 18-gauge wire for hollyhocks or long-stemmed roses in order to achieve the erect bearing that is characteristic of those flowers. For the rest of the flower designs in this book, I use a medium-weight 20-gauge wire, which produces a more relaxed, natural-looking stem. I tend to avoid using really lightweight wire for two reasons: I can't find it in a paper-covered version, and it droops too much from the weight of the flowers.

If you plan to work with wire, you'll need a wire cutter. A basic wire cutter like the one I use can be purchased in most craft and hardware stores. This tool is handy for cutting the really thick 18-gauge wire. Sometimes I can get away with using a crummy pair of scissors to cut the thinner 20-gauge wire, but cutting wire with scissors will simply ruin your scissors.

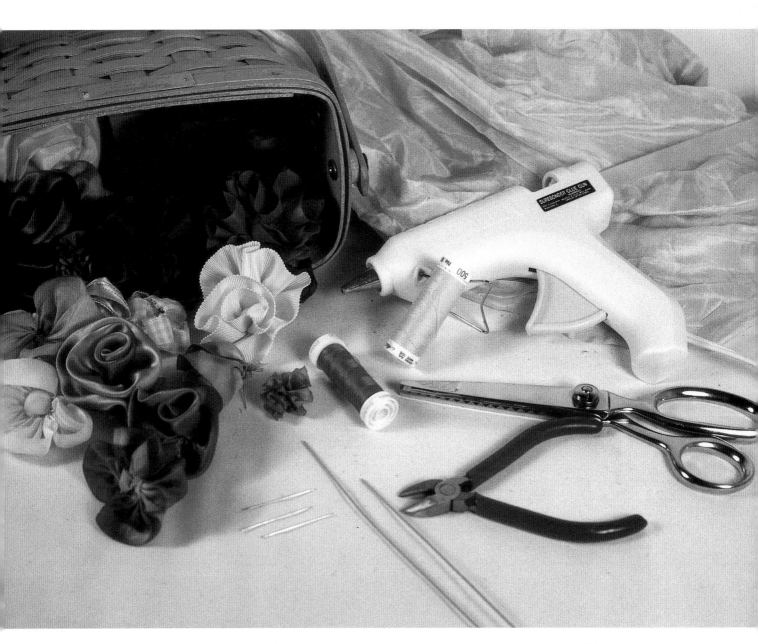

Storage Box or Basket. I mentioned earlier that I usually make flowers without having a specific project in mind, so I have to store them in a nice covered basket so they won't get crushed while I figure out how I'm going to use them. Then when I feel like creating a project, I take out my basket and browse through the "garden." This strategy really works for me because I don't need a reason to make flowers—I can do it just for the fun of it and enjoy the beautiful results. Also, if you like to experiment with widths and lengths of ribbon, you can store the flowers in your box, and eventually you'll find yourself using even the ones you don't like, proving the notion that there's no such thing as a "bad" flower.

An assortment of supplies for making ribbon flowers: needles, thread, wire, wire cutters, scissors, glue gun, glue sticks, and a basket for storing finished flowers.

Making Ribbon Flowers, Step by Step

Preparing Your Ribbons

Before you can begin working with your ribbons, there are some steps you may need to take to prepare them.

RINSING

Hand-dyed ribbon sometimes retains excess color that wasn't set into the fabric during the dyeing process. In order to avoid any unwanted bleeding of color when the ribbon comes in contact with water—even exposure to rain or snow can cause the color to run—rinse it by hand in cool water before using it. Let the ribbon stand in the water for 10 minutes, then change the water and repeat until traces of the dye are no longer visible. Air-dry the rinsed ribbon on a line or rack; the ribbon may fray if it's dried in the clothes dryer. If you suspect that a ribbon you've purchased was hand-dyed, rinse it before you use it.

PRESSING

If your newly purchased or rinsed ribbons are wrinkled, you should press them so that the creases won't detract from your flower designs. Try to identify the fabric the ribbon is made from first, as too hot an iron could melt polyester, scorch silk, or ruin velvet. Pressing—starting with a cool iron, and gently gliding the iron over the ribbon—is less likely to damage ribbon than ironing, or actively pulling the creases out of the ribbon with a hot iron. Avoid stretching the ribbon as you press it. Silk is especially elastic and can easily lose its shape.

Always start by pressing the wrong side of the ribbon (if there is a wrong side) with the iron on its lowest setting. If the creases are resistant, gradually increase the heat until the ribbon cooperates, or use a pressing cloth, which protects the ribbon from the hot iron and keeps it from getting pulled out of shape.

Always rinse hand-dyed ribbons in cool water to ensure that all excess dye has been removed. Gently press badly wrinkled ribbons before working with them, using a pressing cloth if needed.

Basting

Basting is a straight line of long, loose, in-and-out stitches. It is different from other kinds of stitching in that both the stitches and the spaces between them are large. Although basting is most commonly used to hold something in place temporarily while sewing a garment or other item, it is the primary sewing technique for creating ribbon flowers, because it allows the ribbon to be gathered easily.

The smallest basting stitches should be about ¼ inch long, with spaces of approximately ¼ to ½ inch between them. If the stitches are too small or too close together, gathering the ribbon will be difficult, if not impossible. Even more important than the size and spacing of the stitches is their alignment: They must lie in a relatively straight line. While it is acceptable for stitches to wander slightly, zigs, zags, curves, and changes of direction should be avoided unless indicated in the instructions. Ribbon is basted either down the center or along its edge, depending on the design. When basting along an edge, baste as close to it as you can without

falling off, regardless of the ribbon's width. Almost without exception, you should use doubled thread—it makes for a more stable result. Thread the needle with about 1 yard of thread, fold it in half, then double-knot the ends together.

Basting is usually done by hand, but almost all of the flowers in this book can be basted either by hand or on a sewing machine. So that the machine will gather the ribbon automatically as you stitch it, set your baste stitch to wide and your tension to high, from 7 through 9. When machine-sewing silk or other finely woven fabrics, use a needle specifically made for machine basting on finer fabrics, which should be noted on the package.

As I mentioned earlier, the peony (or modified rose) and poppy designs could also be done using wire-edge ribbon without having to baste at all. Just push the ribbon along one of the wires so that it gathers, then manipulate and tack the ribbon according to the instructions before removing or cutting the exposed wire.

In addition to ribbon color, texture, and width, the size and spacing of the stitches can affect the look of your flower. (Above) Three roses are being made here. The wire-edge ribbon is gathered along one of the wires instead of folded and basted. The medium-width apricot ribbon is basted and gathered tightly, while the wide white fabric is basted and gathered loosely. (Right) Each set of variables creates a unique flower, though all can be identified as roses.

Creating
with Ribbon

Being creative is an inherent part of being human. In order to get in touch with our creative selves, we must make an effort to engage in activities that force us to think imaginatively and offer opportunities to gain confidence. When you're able to make design decisions with deliberation and self-assurance, you're more likely to show and share the results with others, rather than hide them in your closet.

There are two strategies for crafting or making art: copying someone else's ideas, and creating based on one's own ideas. Originality is certainly more

difficult than imitation, but it's also far more rewarding. Copying is a good way to learn how to make creative decisions and to strengthen creative "muscles." Start by making a variety of flowers, first by reproducing some of the examples that are shown in this book, then by experimenting with other colors, widths, and textures of ribbon. As you work through this process, you will learn to assess which combinations are appealing and compelling to you. Eventually, you will create unique flowers that reflect your personal style of expression.

An exquisite dark-to-light arrangement of flowers.

EXERCISE: GETTING IN TOUCH WITH YOUR CREATIVE ENERGY

When I first began crafting, how to begin a piece was a mystery to me. As I gained experienced, I was able to devise a simple technique to help smooth the way.

Start by deciding what kind of project you want to make—wearable, gift, or something to commemorate a special occasion. Then take out your finished flowers and leaves. As I mentioned earlier, I like to make flowers using many different sizes, shapes, colors, and textures of ribbon, whenever the urge strikes and without a thought as to where or how they'll be used. When I'm ready to make a project, I take out my basket of flowers and begin.

This is not the time for distractions like television or people. You need to make some quiet time for yourself. (Early in the morning and late at night are best if you have a house full of people.) When all is quiet, become aware of your hands, focusing your attention on them for several minutes. This part of the exercise helps connect your conscious mind to your creative self. You might feel your hands become a little warmer, or maybe even vibrate a little. This technique takes practice, so don't get discouraged. Once you're able to focus attention on your hands, gradually try to expand that awareness to the rest of your body as you continue the exercise.

Begin sorting your flowers based on color. Perhaps you can start by making a simple color wheel (see page 15). If you don't have enough colors to make a wheel, or if you don't have all six colors with the same level of intensity—a real possibility if you're a beginner—then make a grouping consisting of several values of the same color. Choose a single flower, using it as your main color, then place it on a neutral background.

This project unifies extremes of contrast in color and value with dazzling results.

Consider what kind of emphasis you want to create within your arrangement. Do you want to work from light to dark, or from dark to light? Search through your flowers, looking for tints, shades, and tones of your main color. Stay in touch with your creative energy by continuing to concentrate on your hands.

Move your selection of flowers to the surface of the project and lay them out in a design that you like and that seems appropriate for the piece. Then ask yourself the following questions, which are meant to be critical in a constructive way:

- How does the size of each flower affect the layout? Is something too large or too small? Does the arrangement seem balanced?

- Do the textures and colors complement each other? Do I need to make any of the flowers smaller because the color and/or texture of the ribbon overpowers the other elements?

- Do I need to make more flowers in order to complete the value scale/color scheme?

- Should I add stemmed flowers to create variety?

By exploring through trial and error what doesn't work, you will discover what *does* work. Watch what happens when you add something, or take something away. You may begin to "hear" the piece "telling" you where to put a particular flower. Don't

be alarmed—this peculiar sensation just means that you're in touch with the naturally creative part of yourself. If you keep focusing on your hands and making color choices by following the guidelines on pages 14–17, all the while having fun, you will create something that reflects your unique essence.

When all of the flowers are in place, begin adding leaves, asking yourself the same kinds of questions as you try various combinations and configurations. Keep in mind that the visual weight of each flower/leaf pair should be similar. Leaves are a good place to explore texture, but only as long as they remain visually equal or subordinate to the flowers.

When you feel that all of the elements are in harmony, glue or tack them in place according to the project instructions. To attach flowers to a wearable, simply tack them on with a few stitches, or apply them with Velcro so that they can be removed when the garment is cleaned. (See page 80 for more information.)

STORING FINISHED PROJECTS

Store your completed projects in boxes to keep the flowers from getting crushed. If the ribbons somehow lose their shape, steaming or pressing may help remedy the problem. Avoid wetting any velvet ribbons in the arrangement. Dry cleaning may work in that case, but check with your dry cleaner first to be sure.

All three of these attractive color combinations simultaneously express the principles of harmony and contrast.

Ribbon

Flower

Designs

Posies

The first flower design is the simplest. All that's required to make a posey is to baste the ribbon right down the middle, gather it into a fluffy mass, and tack it in place at the back. The result is a full, puffy flower that's great as a "filler" or as an accent, and yet is pretty enough to stand alone.

I usually make my posies with narrow ribbon—for the demonstration, I used ribbon that's 25mm (about 1 inch) wide—but wider ribbon can also be used. Regardless of width, the softer the ribbon, the fluffier the posey. Note that wire-edge ribbon cannot be used to make a posey.

SKILL LEVEL

Beginner

TIME REQUIRED

10 minutes per flower

SUPPLIES

No more than 12 inches of ⅝- to 1-inch-wide soft-edge ribbon or fabric
Thinner widths require less ribbon or fabric

General-purpose needle and thread
Use a milliner's needle for lightweight fabrics such as silk and organdy

(Above) *A black-and-yellow check posey made from Mokuba "Cupra" (ribbon #4718, color #5).* (Right) *A posey made from ⅝-inch-wide Hanah Silk in "periwinkle."*

1. Baste the ribbon right down the center of its width. Hold the basting thread in one hand and use the other to gather the ribbon by scrunching it down the length of thread.

2. Finger-press and fluff the gathered ribbon into the shape of a ball.

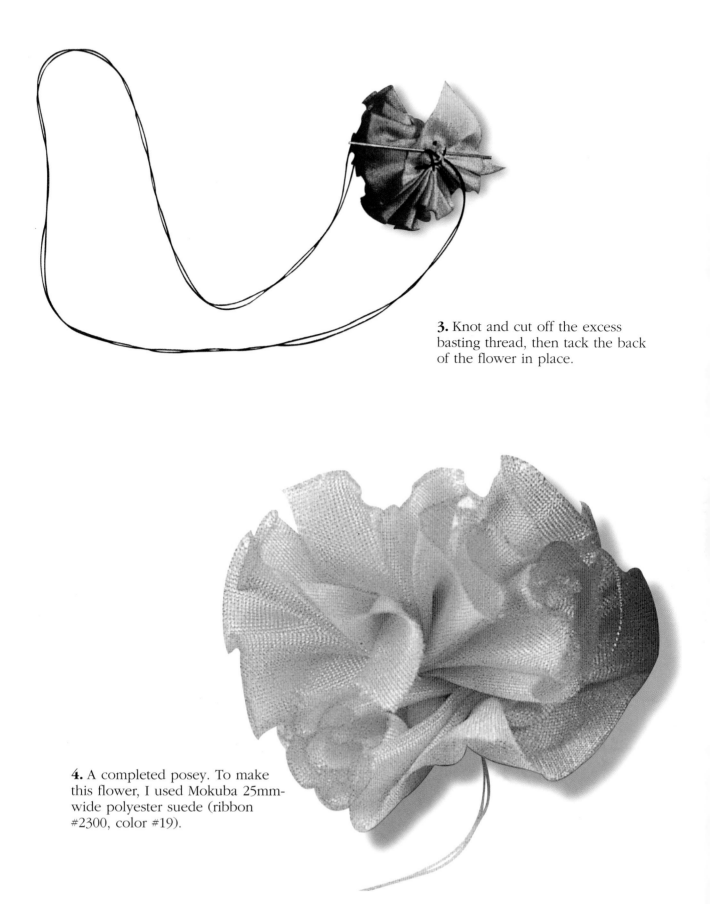

3. Knot and cut off the excess basting thread, then tack the back of the flower in place.

4. A completed posey. To make this flower, I used Mokuba 25mm-wide polyester suede (ribbon #2300, color #19).

Peonies

The peony is lots of fun to make because it's virtually impossible to get an unattractive result. With this flower, we switch from basting straight down the middle of the ribbon to basting down from one corner at a 45-degree angle to the opposite selvedge, straight along that selvedge, then back up again at 45 degrees to the opposite corner. Then just gather and roll, tacking each roll as you go.

The peony design looks most beautiful with edge-dyed ribbon because the unbasted selvedge of the ribbon is accentuated in the finished flower. I usually make peonies with 1½-inch-wide ribbon, but ribbon up to 8 inches wide can be used. If you need extra-large flowers for chair bows or large centerpieces, start with 4-inch-wide ribbon, which creates an opulent magnolia-style flower.

SKILL LEVEL

Beginner

TIME REQUIRED

15 minutes per flower

SUPPLIES

1 yard of 1½-inch-wide soft-edge or wire-edge ribbon
Widths from 1 to 8 inches may be used. Wider widths require more ribbon or fabric; narrower ones, less

General-purpose needle and thread
Use a milliner's needle for lightweight fabrics such as silk and organdy

(Above) *A peony pin made from Hanah Silk 1½-inch-wide variegated "briar rose."* (Right) *A pink peony made from Mokuba 1½-inch-wide suede ribbon.*

1. Examine the ribbon to determine which side is the "right" side. If the ribbon is variegated or multicolored, decide which selvedge should appear in the peony's center. (Note that the *unbasted* selvedge will become the center of the flower.)

Bring the needle and thread up through the back of the ribbon at the corner of the cut edge opposite the selvedge that will be basted. Working from the corner down to the basting selvedge, make the first few basting stitches at a 45-degree angle (but in a straight line), then continue stitching straight along the selvedge. When you reach the end of the ribbon, angle the last few stitches at 45 degrees so that they end at the corner of the opposite cut edge.

2. Hold the basting thread in one hand and use the other to gather the ribbon by scrunching it down the length of thread. The more gathered the ribbon, the fuller your peony will be. Do not tie off the end of the basting thread.

3. Starting at the end of the ribbon where you started basting, roll it once, then tack the roll in place at the very bottom. This is the center of your peony.

4. Continue spiraling the gathered ribbon around the center, tacking each spiral on or above the baste line. (This is done not only to keep the center from popping out, but so that the stitching won't show on the front of the flower.) Poke the needle all the way through the material to ensure that the center is secure. When it becomes difficult to push the needle through the center, push it through as close to the center as possible. If you run out of thread, just tie off, rethread the needle, and continue tacking.

5. Keep checking the top of the flower to make sure you're happy with the way it looks. When you're done, tie off the basting thread and tack the end of the ribbon to the center of the underside in order to cover your stitching.

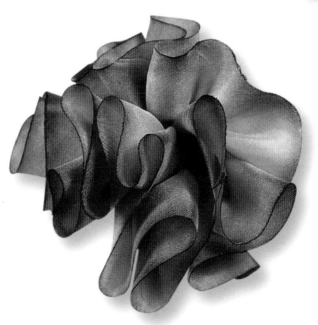

6. A completed peony.

Roses

This design, another baste-along-the-edge flower, makes a classic American Beauty–style rose. The rose is basted and rolled similarly to the peony (see pages 36–37), but the ribbon is folded and the selvedges are basted so that the fold is highlighted in the finished flower. The degree to which the ribbon is gathered can be varied to produce a range of looks. Loose gathers yield more of a spiraled rose, while tight gathers create a swirl of lavish petals.

SKILL LEVEL

Beginner

TIME REQUIRED

1 hour per flower

SUPPLIES

1 yard of 2½-inch-wide soft-edge or wire-edge ribbon or fabric
Widths from 1 to 8 inches may be used. Wider widths require more ribbon or fabric; narrower ones, less

General-purpose needle and thread
Use a milliner's needle for lightweight fabrics such as silk and organdy

A ravishing array of roses. (Above, right) Hanah Silk 2½-inch-wide in "mango ice." (Above) Renaissance Ribbon wire-edge pink-and-violet variegated. (Right) White satin fabric cut on the bias into a wide strip.

1. Examine the ribbon to determine which side is the "right" side. (Note that the *center* of the ribbon's width will be the most prominent in the completed rose because the ribbon is folded.) Fold the ribbon in half selvedge to selvedge so that the right side is showing. Do not press or iron it. If you're working with wire-edge ribbon, don't fold it; just gather one of its selvedges along the wire and proceed to step 3.

Bring the needle and thread up through the ribbon at the corner of a folded edge. Working from that corner down to the selvedges, make the first few basting stitches at a 45-degree angle (but in a straight line), then continue stitching straight along the selvedges. As you approach the other cut end of the ribbon, angle the last few stitches at 45 degrees so that they end at the corner of the folded edge. Do not tie off or knot the thread.

2. Hold the basting thread in one hand and use the other to gather the ribbon on the thread. Decide how ruffled you would like your rose to be by adjusting the gathers. You can tie off the basting thread at this point, or you can wait until the very end, which gives you the option of adjusting the gathers as you roll the ribbon.

3. Starting at the end where you began basting, roll the ribbon once to create the central bud, then tack it in place at the baste line.

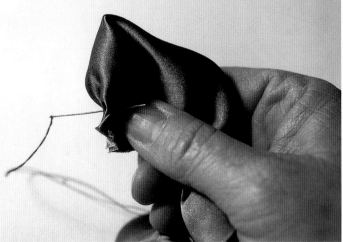

4. Continue spiraling the gathered ribbon around the bud, tacking each spiral at or above the baste line. This technique not only keeps the center from popping out, but it also prevents the stitching from showing on the front of the flower. Poke your needle all the way through the ribbon to ensure that the center is secure. When it becomes difficult to push the needle all the way through the center, push it through as close to the center as possible.

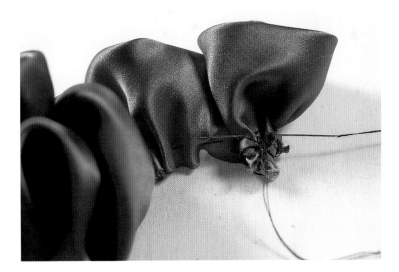

5. As you work, keep checking the top of the flower to make sure it's looking right. If you run out of thread, just knot it off, rethread the needle, and continue tacking.

6. Complete your rose by tacking the end of the ribbon to the center of the underside in order to cover your stitching.

Hollyhocks

There are many varieties of hollyhock, but the one I love most is the double hollyhock. This flower design is similar to the peony and the rose, except that the ribbon is folded in half and basted on the fold, creating a full yet shallow bloom. Real hollyhocks come in a wide range of colors, offering flowermakers an opportunity to use many different ribbons and still get a natural-looking result, though the lighter the weight of your ribbon or fabric, the more authentic your flowers will look. Variegated and edge-dyed ribbons are especially well suited to hollyhocks, as both selvedges of the ribbon are emphasized in the finished flower. Because a hollyhock comprises a stalk of several blooms as well as some scallop-shaped leaves, I've included instructions for assembling one. Note that the hollyhock cannot be made with wire-edge ribbon.

SKILL LEVEL

Beginner/Intermediate

TIME REQUIRED

10 minutes per bloom (leaves, stem, and assembly additional)

SUPPLIES

For the fuller flowers: Three or four 18- to 27-inch lengths of 2½-inch-wide soft-edge ribbon or fabric

For the smaller flowers: Two or three 18- to 20-inch lengths of 1-inch-wide soft-edge ribbon or fabric

For the larger scalloped leaves: Ten 9-inch lengths of 1½-inch-wide soft-edge ribbon

For the smaller scalloped leaves: Five 4-inch lengths of 1-inch-wide soft-edge ribbon

General-purpose needle and thread
Use a milliner's needle for lightweight fabrics such as silk and organdy

For the stem: At least 12 inches of 7/16-inch-wide ribbon
You may need more, depending on the length of the stem

12 inches of 18-gauge paper-covered florist's wire

Glue gun and glue

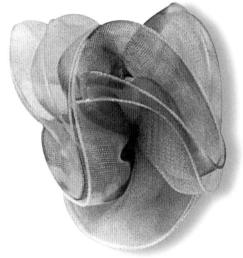

Both the green-and-light-apricot variegated organdy bloom (color #4881) (above) and the navy blue checked velvet bloom (right) are made with Mokuba ribbon.

1. Start by making the flowers, working with the wider ribbon first. Examine the ribbon to determine which side is the "right" side. (Note that the selvedges of the ribbon are the most prominent in a hollyhock bloom.) Fold the ribbon in half lengthwise so that the *wrong* side is showing. Do not press or iron it.

Bring the needle and thread up through the ribbon at one corner of the unfolded edge. Working from that corner down to the folded edge, make the first few basting stitches at a 45-degree angle (but in a straight line), then continue stitching straight along the folded edge. When you reach the other end of the ribbon, angle the last few stitches at a 45-degree angle so that they end at the opposite corner of the unfolded edge.

Hold the basting thread in one hand and use the other to gather the ribbon by scrunching it down the length of thread. Start at the end of the ribbon where you began basting, gathering it tightly to produce a pronounced ruffle. So that you're still able to adjust the gathers as you roll the ribbon in the next step, don't knot off the thread yet.

2. Tightly fold the first ruffle in half, then tack it in place at the baste line. Continue gathering the ribbon tightly, then folding and tacking each ruffle at or above the baste line, which keeps the center ruffle from popping out and prevents the stitching from showing on the front of the flower. Poke your needle all the way through the ribbon to ensure that the center is secure. When it becomes difficult to push it all the way through the center, push it through as close to the center as possible. As you work, keep checking the top of the flower to make sure it's looking right. If you run out of thread, just knot it off, rethread the needle, and continue tacking.

3. To complete the bloom, knot and cut off the excess basting thread, then tack the back of the flower in place.

4. Repeat steps 1 through 3 to make two or three more large flowers with the wider ribbon, then two or three smaller flowers with the narrower ribbon. To make the leaves, follow the instructions on page 76. Start by making five large and three small leaves. To make the stem, follow the instructions on pages 70–71, but instead of leaving 3 inches of the wire uncovered at the top of the stem, wrap the entire length of wire with ribbon.

To assemble the stalk, apply glue close to the bottom of the stem. Orient a large leaf so that it's facing right side up, then wrap the basted area around the stem where you applied the glue. Glue a large flower to the stem slightly above the leaf, wrapping it around the stem. Repeat, alternating between leaves and blooms and progressing from large leaves and flowers to small ones as you work your way up the stem. You may find it necessary to make more leaves as you create your stalk.

5. A completed hollyhock stalk. The flowers and leaves are made with two widths of Hanah Silk in "garnet" and "mossy rock."

Chrysanthemums

The chrysanthemum is a loop-style flower that can be made with either soft-edge or wire-edge ribbon. I prefer to use the wire-edge ribbon with this design for two reasons. First, it's much easier to manipulate; second, chrysanthemums made with soft-edge ribbon look more like elaborate bows than flowers (see below for two examples of these). If you would like to use soft-edge ribbon, use a narrow width to start. Experiment with both types to decide which one better suits your working style and personal taste, as well as the needs of your project.

SKILL LEVEL

Beginner/Intermediate

TIME REQUIRED

20 minutes per flower

SUPPLIES

24 inches of ¾-inch-wide soft-edge or wire-edge ribbon
Widths from ¼ to 1 inch may be used. Wider widths require more ribbon or fabric; narrower ones, less

General-purpose needle and thread
Use a milliner's needle for lightweight fabrics such as silk and organdy

(Left) *Better Homes & Gardens 3mm-wide red.* (Above) *Hanah Silk ⁷⁄₁₆-inch-wide in "copper patina."*

Dear Mom,
Happy Birthday
With Love,
Deborah

1. Fold the ribbon into 1¼-inch sections, finger-pressing them in place. (It isn't necessary to be precise about the size of the folds as long as they're all the same size.) If needed or desired, pin the folds in place.

2. Baste the ribbon in place along one side of the folds.

3. Gather the ribbon, then manipulate the folds so that they lie flat and are aligned on the basted edge in a straight line. You may need to work the ribbon into a few configurations, such as the fan shape shown here, in order to do this.

4. Work the aligned folds into a tight, circular bud. Tack the bud in place at the base, poking the needle all the way through every layer of ribbon and turning the bud as you tack it so that the base supports and connects all of the petals.

5. Open the folds and shape them into the chrysanthemum's petals. Push down the tops of the center petals so that they look more rounded and flowerlike.

6. A chrysanthemum made with Renaissance Ribbons 16mm-wide "Taffetas Ombre Laitonné" wire-edge (ribbon #8051, color #11).

Pansies

The pansy is another baste-along-the-edge design, but instead of using one single length of ribbon, this flower uses two same-size pieces of ribbon arranged in an L shape. Variegated and edge-dyed ribbon, which I used in the demonstration, make this design look more realistic. Experiment by positioning the contrasting edge on the outside of the petals rather than in the center, by working with patterned ribbon or fabric, or even velvet or chiffon. (Note that wire-edge ribbon can't be used with this design.) You can also explore some unusual possibilities by trying out a variety of centers. For more information, see "Flower Centers," pages 64–69.

SKILL LEVEL

Intermediate/Advanced

TIME REQUIRED

20 minutes per flower

SUPPLIES

For a 2-inch-wide pansy with a French knot center

Four 4-inch-long pieces of 1-inch-wide soft-edge ribbon or fabric

1- to 3-inch-long piece of ⅝-inch-wide (or narrower) soft-edge ribbon or fabric in a complementary color

Thread
Color should match the center of the flower

General-purpose needle
Use a milliner's needle for lightweight fabrics such as silk and organdy

An arrangement of fanciful pansies. (Clockwise from top) *Mokuba 36mm-wide rayon/nylon checked velvet (ribbon #4524, color #26) with a multiple French knot center; Mokuba polyester/rayon blend velvet (ribbon #2500, color #52) with a squiggly center; and Mokuba 75mm-wide nylon (ribbon #1500) with a vintage button center.*

1. If your ribbon is variegated or multicolored, decide which of its selvedges you would like to appear in the center of the flower. (Note that the *basted* selvedge will become the center of the flower, so choose the color of the thread accordingly.) To make one side of your pansy, arrange two of the flower ribbons in an L shape, with the horizontal piece overlapping the vertical one.

2. Begin basting at the top righthand corner of the L's vertical stem. Work the stitches in a gentle curve from the corner down to the opposite selvedge, then continue stitching straight along the selvedge. When you reach the horizontal piece of ribbon, curve the stitches until you reach its bottom outside edge. Baste straight along the selvedge once more, then work the last few stitches in a curve so that they end at the top righthand corner of the horizontal stem.

　To make the other side of your pansy, repeat steps 1 and 2 using the other two pieces of flower ribbon.

3. To make a set of pansy petals, pick up one of the basted L shapes, hold the basting thread in one hand, and use the other to gather the ribbon by scrunching it down the length of thread. Tie off the thread so that the petals stay in place. Repeat with the other basted L shape. You should now have two double-petaled pieces.

4. Hold the petals together by the gathered corners of the L shapes. Turn the petals upside down, then tack them together to form a flower.

5. Hand-press the flower open and decide which kind of center you want. (See pages 65–69 for instructions on how to add button, ribbon, and polymer clay centers.) In this example, I used a single French knot center, which is made by tying a short piece of narrow ribbon into a loose knot, cutting the tails from the knot, then tacking the knot to the center of the pansy.

6. Three completed pansies with French knot centers.

Poppies

The design for the poppy is a baste-along-the-edge design, but with one important difference: The length of the ribbon is shorter, and the ribbon is gathered only in the center, then flattened to create a broad flower. This technique is tricky, but working with softer ribbon makes it a little easier. (An alternate method is given at the end of step 5.) Note that the basted and gathered edge becomes the center of the flower, so edge-dyed and variegated ribbons are good choices for making poppies.

If you want to stem your poppies, a lightweight wire will give you that authentic "floppy poppy" look. For more information, see "Stems," page 70.

SKILL LEVEL

Intermediate/Advanced

TIME REQUIRED

15 minutes per flower

SUPPLIES

18 inches of 1½-inch-wide soft-edge ribbon or fabric
Widths from 1 to 3½ inches may be used. Wider widths require more ribbon or fabric; narrower ones, less

General-purpose needle and thread
Use a milliner's needle for lightweight fabrics such as silk and organdy

An array of poppies in a medley of ribbons. (Clockwise from top left) Mokuba 50mm-wide nylon/polyester blend (ribbon #4595), Mokuba 50mm-wide polyester/rayon velvet (ribbon #2500), Offray 1½-inch-wide "Lady Chiffon" polyester/nylon blend in "tulip," and Hanah Silk 1½-inch-wide in variegated "briar rose."

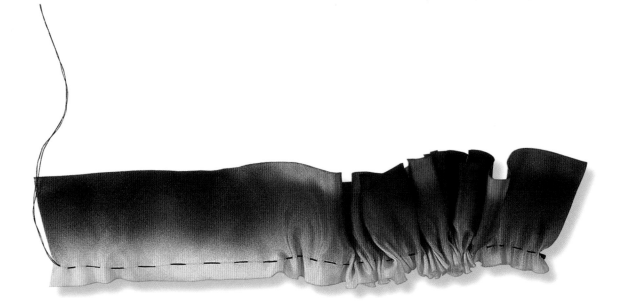

1. Examine the ribbon to determine which is the right side; if the ribbon is variegated or multicolored, decide which selvedge you want to be the center of the poppy. (Note that the *basted* selvedge will become the center of the flower.) Using doubled thread, baste along the selvedge of the ribbon, bringing the thread up through the front of the ribbon so that the knot is at the back. Gather the ribbon on the thread but avoid scrunching it too tightly, which will distort the end where the basting thread is knotted. (The ends need to be matched in step 3.) Allow the needle and thread to remain attached to the ribbon.

2. Shape the gathered ribbon into a semicircle, then take a few more stitches parallel to the cut end, finishing on the wrong side of the ribbon.

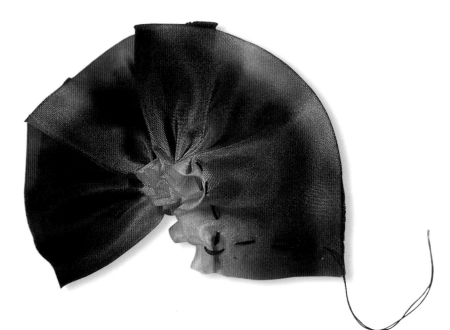

3. Bring the right sides of the ribbon ends together, pin them in place, then baste them together to create a tiny seam, again leaving the needle and thread attached.

4. Turn the flower over, then poke the gathers through to the front.

5. Distribute the ruffles of the center evenly. While holding the stitches at the seam flat, carefully pull the thread to tighten the gathers and reduce the size of the center. Knot off the thread to complete the flower.

NOTE: If the thread doesn't pull smoothly, you probably crossed your stitches when you switched from basting along the selvedge to basting along the ends. You can avoid this problem by basting the length of the ribbon, then stitching the ends together with a different needle and thread before pushing through the center and tightening the gathers with the original basting thread.

Daisies

The daisy is the most challenging design in this book. If you're a beginner, I recommend that you tackle it only after trying your hand at some of the easier flowers. The wonderful thing about this daisy is its versatility. You can vary the number of petals from five to eight, or you can make a "half daisy" with just four petals as an accent for a larger flower (see page 81 for an example). You can make a full, puffy flower or a structured, tailored one by adjusting your basting technique. By carefully choosing colors and fabrics, you can make other multipetaled flowers such as a black-eyed Susan or a dahlia. The center provides yet another opportunity for you to express your creativity. Note that wire-edge ribbon can't be used for this design.

(see page 81 for an example)

SKILL LEVEL

Advanced

TIME REQUIRED

20 minutes per flower

SUPPLIES

For a 2-inch-wide flower

18 inches of 1½-inch-wide soft-edge ribbon or fabric
Widths from 1 to 4 inches may be used. Wider widths require more ribbon or fabric; narrower ones, less

A large button in a complementary color

General-purpose needle and thread
Use a milliner's needle for lightweight fabrics such as silk and organdy

A daisy can wear many colors. (Above) A daisy without folded edges made with Mokuba burgundy ribbon with copper-colored metallic edging and a squiggly center. (Right) A folded-edge daisy made with Hanah Silk 1½-inch-wide in "black-eyed Susan" with a polymer clay center.

1. Examine the ribbon to determine which side is the "right" side; if it's variegated or multicolored, decide which of its selvedges you would like to appear in the center of the flower. (Note that the *basted* selvedge will become the center of the flower, and that you'll be basting on the *wrong* side of the ribbon.)

Iron or finger-press the ribbon into fifths, sixths, sevenths, or eighths, depending on how many petals you want. (For this demonstration I made a 7-petal daisy, but only part of the ribbon is visible here.) If you want your petals to look more defined, fold back ¼ inch of the selvedge opposite the baste line, then iron or finger-press it in place.

2. Start basting at the top righthand corner of the ribbon, making sure to catch the ¼-inch fold in the first stitch. Work the stitches straight down along the cut end of the ribbon, then along the selvedge. When you reach the first fold line, baste along one side of it to the top of the ribbon (including the ¼-inch fold), then reverse the stitches down along the other side of the fold line back to the selvedge. Repeat until the entire length of ribbon is basted. You should finish basting at the top lefthand corner of the other cut end of the ribbon. Do not cut or knot off the thread.

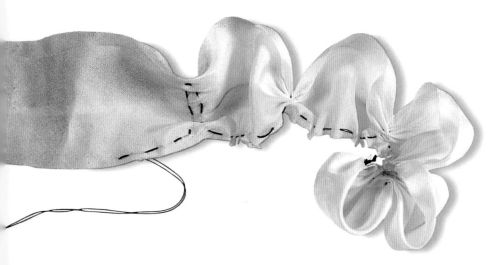

3. Hold the basting thread in one hand and use the other to gently gather the ribbon on the thread. As the petals begin to form, distribute them evenly on the basting thread.

4. Shape the petals into a semicircle or U shape, then stitch the ends of the ribbon together without knotting off the thread.

5. Distribute the petals on the thread in order to create a more or less symmetrical circle. When you're satisfied with the way the petals are laying, tack the ends of the ribbon together, then tack the petals in place at the center of the daisy.

6. Complete the daisy by attaching a center. (Refer to pages 64–69 for instructions on how to make button, ribbon, and polymer clay centers.) This example features a large cloth-covered button.

Finishing Your Flowers

Flower Centers

Two of the flower designs in this book—the pansy and the daisy—require the addition of a center. The poppy, which has its own gathered center, can also be embellished with an additional center. It's said that necessity is the mother of invention, and these designs can offer you an opportunity to use your imagination and bring them to life with buttons, ribbons, or your own original polymer clay creations. Depending on your mood or the needs of your project, you can make a flower look whimsical, fantastic, or just like the real thing.

A multicolored arrangement of organza daisies made with Mokuba ribbon, finished with with button and short ribbon tassel centers.

BUTTONS

A button is the all-around simplest flower center. Even if you don't have a sewing basket, you're sure to have a few stray buttons squirreled away in a draw that you can use as centers. Buttons are also the easiest to attach— just sew them on with matching thread as you would for a shirt or blouse, and you're done.

These shimmering organza daisies feature simple blouse button centers.

Instead of limiting your button search to the bottom of your junk drawer, you can look for unusual vintage and novelty buttons in antique stores and flea markets.

RIBBONS

Ribbon centers are a little more challenging than buttons, but are accessible even to beginning sewers. I like to make a variety of ribbon centers, including the French knot, the squiggly, and the mini-tassel. You'll need a selection of narrow ribbons—about ½ inch wide or less—for all three techniques.

French Knot. Not to be confused with the classic embroidery stitch, my French knot is just a very easy-to-make ribbon center. Simply tie a loose knot in the middle of a 1- to 3-inch-long piece of narrow ribbon, cut off the tails, then tack into place.

Just tie a loose knot in a short piece of ribbon . . .

. . . then cut off the tails and tack in the center. For these pansies, I used ⁷⁄₁₆-inch-wide Hanah Silk in "Midas touch."

You can use a single French knot or several, depending on the size of your flower.

The Squiggly. A squiggly center is just what it sounds like: a length of narrow novelty ribbon, trim, or fabric spiraled in the center of the flower, then haphazardly tacked or glued into place.

Squiggly centers can be pleated and opaque and arranged in a neat coil . . .

. . . or sheer and glittery and loosely scrunched, as long as they contrast with the petals and provide a touch of uniqueness.

Mini-Tassel. Slightly more elaborate in appearance than the French knot and the squiggly, the mini-tassel is actually very easy to make.

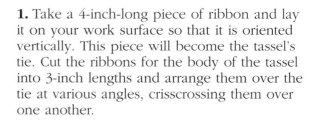

1. Take a 4-inch-long piece of ribbon and lay it on your work surface so that it is oriented vertically. This piece will become the tassel's tie. Cut the ribbons for the body of the tassel into 3-inch lengths and arrange them over the tie at various angles, crisscrossing them over one another.

2. Take the ends of the tie and cross one over the other . . .

3. . . . then tie the ribbons together in the center with a double knot.

4. Tack the tassel's knot into the center of the flower. You can dress up a tassel by adding a bead at the top.

POLYMER CLAY

Polymer clay is a plastic-based material composed of particles of polyvinyl chloride (PVC) suspended in a plasticizer. Polymer clay is soft and malleable at room temperature, but upon heating the PVC particles fuse into a hard plastic. In contrast to objects made from traditional earth-based clays, which often require multiple firings at high temperatures, polymer clay creations need only be heated in a household oven for a short time and at a low temperature, usually for only 20 minutes at about 275°F.

Polymer clay is made by several manufacturers and is available in a wide range of colors and textures, including metallic, iridescent, and stone. If you've worked with polymer clay previously, you can use any technique you like to create flower centers. If you're new to the medium, follow this simple recipe using a soft, easy-to-handle clay such as FIMOSOFT, Sculpey Premo, or Cernit:

1. Cut a 2-ounce block of clay into eighths. Condition one small cube by kneading it, first by rolling it into a snake, then into a ball. Gradually shape the ball into a flat, round disk.

2. Texturize the surface of the disk. For a quick-and-easy texture, prick impressions into the disk with a toothpick or pin. For a more dimensional look, condition another cube of clay, squeeze it through a garlic press, then arrange the little clay "worms" on the disk with a toothpick. (Don't use any tools or surfaces you've used with the clay to prepare food.) If desired, you can make the center into a button by piercing it with two holes.

3. Cure your center by baking it according to the manufacturer's instructions. When it has cooled completely, attach it to the flower either with hot glue or by sewing it in place.

The red-violet silk daisies on this gift bag feature yellow polymer clay centers for maximum contrast.

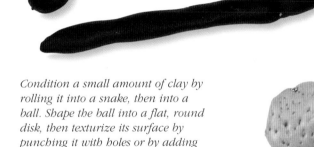

Condition a small amount of clay by rolling it into a snake, then into a ball. Shape the ball into a flat, round disk, then texturize its surface by punching it with holes or by adding small bits of clay.

Stems

Stems allow you to create unique arrangements for home decorating and gift giving. I recommend that you use a heavier, 18-gauge paper-covered wire for substantial flowers like hollyhocks and long-stemmed roses, and medium-weight 20-gauge wire for the rest of the flowers in this book.

1. Load your glue gun with low- or variable-temperature glue, then plug it in. Cut the wire to the desired length. Curve the top inch or so into a U shape, and bend another inch or so below it sideways so that it creates a flat surface. This is where the base of your flower will be glued to the stem.

2. Choose the ribbon for your stem. I use narrow ribbon or fabric, usually 7/16- or 5/8-inch-wide silk, which is easy to apply and yields a smooth surface. Leave the ribbon on the spool as you work with it.

Wrap the entire length of wire with ribbon, leaving a U-shaped bend and a 3-inch length of ribbon at the top.

3. Apply the heated glue to a few inches of the wire along the bottom of the stem. Wrap the ribbon around the wire so that its surface is completely covered. Continue applying glue and wrapping the ribbon around the wire until you reach the bend. Leave about a 3-inch length of ribbon unglued at the top of the stem, then cut the ribbon off the spool.

4. You can attach the flower to the stem using one of two methods. If you don't expect to handle the flower very much, you can simply apply glue to its underside, then press the U shape at the top of the stem into the glue. To finish, fold and glue the extra 3 inches of ribbon to the underside of the flower, making sure that the wire is completely covered. If, on the other hand, you think that the flower will receive alot of handling, use a needle and thread to tack the U shape to the underside of the flower, then tack the extra ribbon into place.

Glue or stitch the U shape to the bottom of the flower, making sure to cover the wire with the extra ribbon.

Leaves

The leaf designs shown below and on the following pages can be used with either stemmed or unstemmed flowers. All you need to decide is which design best complements the shape of your flower. You may want to do a little research before you choose a color, fabric, and shape, either by studying real flowers or looking through reference books and magazines.

EASY LEAVES

Your success with this design will depend on your dexterity with scissors. Note that if these leaves are handled often or roughly, their unfinished edges are likely to fray.

1. Choose a ribbon or fabric for your leaves. In my experience, lighter weights work best because the finished leaves are softer and more translucent, like real leaves. To maximize visual interest, select a variegated ribbon or a printed fabric.

2. Cut a leaf shape out of the ribbon or fabric. If you need a guide for cutting, create a paper or cardboard template, or use a real leaf.

3. To attach an easy leaf to a stem, load and plug in your glue gun, then apply a large drop of glue to the stem. Press the base of the leaf into the glue so that the right side of the ribbon or fabric is facing toward the stem. Fold, twist, and shape the leaf to give it some dimension.

   To attach an easy leaf to the back of a flower, simply tack in place with a needle and thread.

This stemmed poppy features easy leaves made from dark green variegated and pleated velvet ribbons.

FOLDED LEAVES

Folded leaves come in two varieties: the basic version, and the fan. Both can be attached to either stemmed or unstemmed flowers. Use the same ribbon widths for the leaves as you've used for your flowers.

1. To make a basic folded leaf, start with 9 inches of ribbon or fabric. Fold the top lefthand corner down to the center of the opposite selvedge.

2. Repeat with the top righthand corner.

3. Baste through both sides of the ribbon along the unfolded edge.

4. Gather the ribbon on the thread, tie it off, and tack in place at the baste line. You can attach a single folded leaf to the flower or stem.

5. If desired, make a second leaf and stitch them together at the base . . .

6. . . . before tacking or gluing them to the underside of a flower or gluing them to a stem.

1. To make a fan-folded leaf, fold about 9 inches of ribbon or fabric at regular intervals . . .

2. . . . then tack in place along the bottom edge of the folds.

3. Stitch or glue the finished leaf to the underside of a flower, or glue it to a stem.

SCALLOPED LEAVES

This leaf design requires ribbon or fabric in a specific length and width.

1. Baste a 1½-inch-wide by 5-inch-long piece of ribbon in a giant U shape, extending from the top righthand corner, gently curving down to and along the opposite selvedge, then back up to the top lefthand corner.

2. Gather the ribbon on the thread. Shape the ribbon to make a puffy semicircular form, then tie off and tack in place.

3. Stitch or glue the leaf to the underside of a flower, or glue it at its base to a stem.

WIRED LEAVES

The wired leaf is the most challenging leaf design in this book, but it's also the most versatile, as it allows you to make any size or shape leaf you desire. When making wired leaves, always use paper-covered wire in the lightest weight you can find. The width of the ribbon or fabric you use depends on the size of the leaf you want to make.

1. Form the wire into a leaf shape. If you plan to attach the leaf to a stem or insert it into a flower arrangement, add a little extra wire at the base to ensure a secure attachment.

2. Lay a piece of ribbon or fabric right side down on your work surface. Apply heated glue to the shaped wire, place it on the ribbon or fabric, then lay another piece of ribbon or fabric right side up over the wire and press firmly. Hold the "sandwich" up to the light, then cut away the ribbon or fabric about ½ inch from the wire.

3. Stitch or glue the finished leaves to the underside of a flower, glue them to a stem, or simply tuck them in at the bottom of an arrangement.

Wearables and Accessories

Ribbon Flower Corsages

Once you've made some flowers and leaves, you're ready to prove yourself a true artist and proclaim your talent by wearing your own creations. Here are two simple "recipes" for making elegant ribbon flower corsages that can be worn on the lapel or wrist, around the neck on a choker, or as a scarf clasp.

As you create your corsage, choose flowers and leaves that complement the garment, not only its color but the style and weight of its fabric. You can mount your corsage on a clasp-style pin (which can be found at most craft stores) or on a Velcro fastener, or you can sew it directly to the garment. Before permanently attaching your corsage to a garment, consider how the garment will need to be cleaned and whether the fabrics in the corsage can be laundered in the same way. If the fabrics are incompatible and you would rather not mount your corsage on a pin clasp or on Velcro, simply tack the corsage in place with a needle and thread and remove it before laundering the garment.

SIMPLE ROSE CORSAGE

This project combines a single rose with a pair of basic folded leaves. This graceful trio, which takes about an hour to put together, can be worn on many styles of clothing. Your most difficult task will be to find the right ribbon or fabric for your rose—that is, if you don't already have the "perfect" rose hidden away in your storage box or basket. Use lightweight ribbon, since the heavier the ribbon, the harder it is to manipulate.

The procedure is easy: Start by making the rose (see the instructions on pages 40–41), then make the leaves (pages 73–74). Tack the flower to the center point of the two leaves. To complete your corsage, attach a pin clasp by tacking or gluing it to the back of the flower, stitch it to a Velcro fastener, or tack it right on the garment.

A single rose and a pair of folded leaves make a memorable impression.

SKILL LEVEL

Intermediate

TIME REQUIRED

1 hour

SUPPLIES

For the rose: 1 yard of 2½-inch-wide ribbon

For the folded leaves: 10 inches of 2½-inch-wide ribbon
Thinner widths require less ribbon or fabric

General-purpose needle and thread
Use a milliner's needle for lightweight fabrics such as silk and organdy

CORSAGE BOUQUET

A corsage bouquet is an excellent way to dress up a suit or basic dress for an evening business gathering or a formal wedding or party. A bouquet can include several different elements, but so that you're not overwhelmed by too many choices, begin with the background—the color, weight, and texture of the garment on which the bouquet will be worn. Consider which colors and textures of ribbon would provide an interesting yet subtle contrast, then make your selection, keeping in mind that variety will give your bouquet dimension. When I make a bouquet, I use the most sumptuous ribbons I can find so that the end result is always appropriate for an elegant occasion.

This project starts with the largest element, which also serves as the base on which everything else is glued or tacked. Before you glue or stitch anything to your base, evaluate the composition of your bouquet as you make each element, making adjustments and even substitutions as needed. The best way to assess the progress of the bouquet is by holding it against the garment. Finalize your decisions by tacking or gluing only when you're completely satisfied. Note that I used a sturdy pleated velvet ribbon for my base, but if you choose a less substantial fabric you should tack or glue everything to a piece of scrap fabric or crinoline.

1. Following steps 1 through 3 for the chrysanthemum (see pages 48–49), fold the ribbon into the number of "leaves" you want to show along the bottom of your bouquet, baste the folds in place, then arrange them into a fan shape. Remember, you're not making an entire chrysanthemum; you're just folding and stitching the ribbon into a fan. Make sure the fan is not only large enough to hold the other elements but that it will be partially visible as background.

2. Make a half (four-petal) daisy following steps 1 through 5 on pages 60–61. Shape the petals into a half circle instead of a full one, then tack the ends of the ribbon together.

3. Make a rose following the instructions on pages 40–41. The length of ribbon you use will depend on the size of the rose you want. You may use anywhere between 18 and 24 inches of ribbon; I used 20 inches to make the one shown below, left. Check the size of the rose against the chrysanthemum and half daisy, then finish it when it seems in scale with the other elements.

SKILL LEVEL

Intermediate

TIME REQUIRED

1½ hours

SUPPLIES

To make the bouquet shown at right

For the chrysanthemum: 18 inches of 1½-inch-wide ribbon

For the half daisy: 15 inches of 1½-inch-wide ribbon

For the rose: 20 inches of 2½-inch-wide ribbon

For the basic folded leaf: 9 inches of 1-inch-wide ribbon

For the hollyhock: 9 inches of 1½-inch-wide ribbon

For mounting the bouquet (optional): A scrap of fabric or crinoline

For basting the ribbon and tacking the bouquet: General-purpose needle and thread

Glue gun (optional)

If the base ribbon is soft and floppy, or if the base element is small, a corsage bouquet with multiple elements may need to be mounted on a circle of fabric or crinoline.

This corsage bouquet has a somewhat limited palette but features a variety of interesting textures. The chrysanthemum is Mokuba 38mm-wide pleated velvet (ribbon #0500, color #9); the half daisy is Mokuba 1½-inch-wide rayon/polyester (ribbon #4548, color #5); the rose is Hanah Silk 2½-inch-wide satin in "old ivory"; the fan-folded leaf is Hanah Silk 1-inch-wide in "chameleon"; and the hollyhock is Hanah Silk 1½-inch-wide in "moondust."

4. It's possible that your bouquet may seem complete at this point; if so, proceed to step 6. I like my arrangements to feel balanced and thought this one needed a bit of realism, so I used a short length of medium-width variegated green ribbon to make a fan-folded leaf (see page 75).

5. As a final touch, I wanted to harmonize all of the colors in the piece, so I made a small hollyhock bloom (see page 44) using a soft brown silk ribbon edge-dyed with black.

6. Once you've made all the components for your corsage, experiment with a number of different arrangements. Be playful, and don't be afraid to rule something out or add something, even at this point. When you're happy with the design, tack or glue everything into place, then add a clasp pin or Velcro if desired.

If this is your first attempt at making a corsage, keep it simple and make just a two-flower version. Shown here is a rose with a half daisy and a scalloped leaf.

The arrangement of this corsage is similar to the one shown on the preceding page, but the ribbons that were used make the composition seem more elaborate.

"Blooming" Hat

Decorating a hat can be great fun and a wonderful way to explore—and publicize—your creativity. The first step would be to choose a hat that suits your needs. Is the occasion special, like a wedding or a formal party, where you would want to complement a particular outfit? Or do you want a seasonal hat to wear throughout the spring or fall? What kind of statement do you want to make—are you (or is the gathering) fun and funky, elegant and glamorous, or sedate and professional? (If you have trouble finding unadorned hats, refer to page 110 for mail-order sources.) Once you've found just the right hat, focus on your ribbon choices, selecting those that complement the hat as well as the outfit or garment you plan to wear it with.

1. Choose a ribbon for the hatband. In my experience, 1½-inch-wide ribbons work well with most hats—they're prominent without being overpowering—but you may prefer a different width. Wind the ribbon around the crown just above the brim, pull it tightly to make sure that it's flat, then pin it in place. Don't glue or tack on the hatband until you've made all your flowers, because you might decide that its color or texture no longer works with the arrangement you've created.

2. Make flowers and leaves in a range of sizes, keeping in mind that you may not use every single one—or even more than one. That way, you'll have maximum flexibility as you compose your embellishment. Start by laying a large flower on the crown where the hatband's seam will fall. Expand the arrangement by positioning a few smaller flowers and/or leaves around the large one, striving to create balance and visual interest as you consider each combination.

3. When you're satisfied with the result, glue or tack the hatband in place, then the flowers and leaves. Now is the time to add small embellishments—tassels, buttons, beads or pearls, or tiny butterfly or bee charms.

SKILL LEVEL

Intermediate

TIME REQUIRED

2 hours

SUPPLIES

An undecorated hat

Ribbon in a variety of colors and widths

General-purpose needle and thread
Use a milliner's needle for lightweight fabrics such as silk and organdy

Glue gun (optional)

Embellishments (optional)

You can always count on velvet to dress up a casual hat.

This hat's understated color scheme and simple arrangement of ribbon flowers—a single rose and two scalloped leaves—pronounce its wearer as subtle, cool, and delicate.

This hat says "spring has sprung" with a burst of color and texture.

Basket of Flowers Tote

Can't find a venue for all those "leftover" flowers in your storage box or basket? Decorate a sturdy tote or carryall with a gardenful of your blooms. Design your arrangement to fill the entire surface, and don't forget to include a container, stems, and leaves, and maybe even some friendly insects. Compose your design right on the tote, then glue or stitch on the elements when you're sure that the garden is just right. See page 110 for mail-order sources for blank totes.

1. Following the manufacturer's instructions, iron the fusible webbing to the fabric for the container, then cut the container so that it corresponds to the shape of your tote. A short, fat tote should have a short, fat container; a tall, skinny tote should have a tall, skinny one. Peel the backing off the fusible webbing, then position and iron the container on the tote.

2. If you don't have a large reserve of flowers, or if you only have a few, make several in a variety of sizes, shapes, and colors. (You should make more than you need.) Place the flowers on the tote and experiment with a few layouts, visualizing where the stems and leaves would fall.

3. Pin the flowers in place, then glue or tack on the stems, then the flowers, then finally the leaves. As a finishing touch, you can invite a few insect visitors to your garden. (I used two feather butterflies I bought at Wal-Mart.)

Brighten a plain tote with a basket of beautiful spring flowers.

SKILL LEVEL

Advanced

TIME REQUIRED

1½ hours for the flowers

15 minutes for the vase

15 minutes for assembly

SUPPLIES

Plain canvas, cotton, or broadcloth tote or bag

For the container or basket: "Basketweave" print fabric and double-face iron-on fusible webbing

Ribbon in a variety of colors and widths

General-purpose needle and thread
Use a milliner's needle for lightweight fabrics such as silk and organdy

Glue gun (optional)

Embellishments (optional)

Pansy Pouch

Besides being incredibly beautiful, this little pouch is easy to make. It's a charming accessory that can be worn either on a belt or as a pendant, and also makes a great wedding gift as an elegant money holder.

Start by choosing the ribbon or fabric for the pouch. You can use velvet, satin, suede, or cotton—whatever suits the occasion and/or the wearer. When you select the ribbons for the pansies, leaves, strap, and tassels, make sure they complement the pouch fabric's color and texture. I find that Hanah Silk's pansy ribbons, which are available in two color schemes ("wild iris" and "briar rose"), make the most natural-looking pansies. Also, this project is available as a kit from Creative Kits (see the source directory on page 110 for contact information).

SKILL LEVEL

Intermediate/Advanced

TIME REQUIRED

1½ hours

SUPPLIES

For a large pouch (3½ by 4 inches): 10 inches of 100mm-wide ribbon OR a 4- by 10-inch piece of fabric

For a small pouch (1½ by 3 inches): 10 inches of 50mm-wide ribbon OR a 2- by 10-inch piece of fabric

For the pansies: 48 inches of ⅝-inch-wide ribbon

For the leaves: 12 inches of ⅝-inch-wide ribbon

For the strap: Three ⁷⁄₁₆-inch-wide ribbons (use 18-inch lengths for a belt strap and 30-inch lengths for a pendant)

For the mini-tassels (optional): 1 yard each of two ⁷⁄₁₆-inch-wide ribbons

General-purpose needle and thread *Use a milliner's needle for lightweight fabrics such as silk and organdy*

Glue gun (optional)

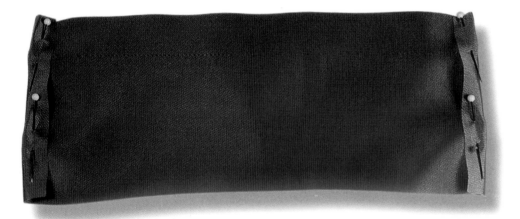

1. Lay the ribbon or fabric for the pouch on your work surface wrong side up. (Two widths of ribbon are shown here—one for a large pouch, the other for a small one.) Fold over and pin ¼ inch at each end, then hand- or machine-stitch in place.

2. Fold the ribbon or fabric to make a 4-inch pouch, then hand- or machine-stitch the edges. This can be done on either the wrong or right side of the pouch; the latter will give you a finished seam, but you will have to turn the pouch inside out once you're finished. (The large pouch was machine-stitched with wrong sides together, while the small pouch was handstitched with right sides together.) The excess ribbon or fabric above the pouch serves as a flap.

3. Make the pansies and leaves following the instructions on pages 52–53 and 73–74 but using the narrower ribbons specified in the materials list on the opposite page. Try several arrangements before gluing or tacking them on.

4. You can make and attach the strap either before or after affixing the flowers and leaves. To make the strap, knot the three ribbons together at least 2 inches from the end, braid them, then knot them again the same length from the other end. Stitch the knots to either side of the pouch, at the top just under the flap. You can also attach some mini-tassels along the bottom and sides of the pouch. (Refer to page 68 for detailed instructions on how to make a mini-tassel.)

This small red velvet pouch is adorned with green-and-red variegated ribbons.

The purple-and-yellow variegated pansies simultaneously contrast and harmonize with this royal blue satin pouch.

Sophisticated and timeless, classic black velvet works with virtually any style and color scheme. The red-and-yellow variegated pansies provide a pretty, graceful touch.

Gifts
and Special
Occasions

Gift Tie-Ons

It's always nice to receive a gift, but a gift embellished with beautiful handmade ribbon flowers is special, since both the giver and the recipient know that the wrapping is unique. You can wrap your gift in paper, of course, but fabric, particularly silk, makes a lasting impression. Even more stunning—and the easiest wrapping of all—are gift bags and baskets, which can be recycled to wrap other gifts or to store precious items. (See the source directory on page 110 for where to find undecorated gift bags.) Whatever wrapping you choose, make sure your ribbon colors coordinate.

1. Create a flower and leaves that complement the wrapping. If you want to include more than one flower, you may need to mount the arrangement on a circle of scrap fabric or crinoline (see "Corsage Bouquet," page 81).

2. Tack or glue a ribbon or other tie to the back of the arrangement, making sure that it's long enough to wrap around the gift and be tied securely. If desired, add a tassel to the bottom of the arrangement, also at the back.

3. Wrap the gift, then tie on your embellishment.

SKILL LEVEL

Beginner

TIME REQUIRED

1 hour

SUPPLIES

See the materials lists for each specific flower and finishing element

General-purpose needle and thread OR glue gun

Undecorated gift bag or basket (optional)

Customize a storage basket for collectibles with ribbon flowers.

For a simple project, find an empty gift bag and make matching flowers.

Give a simple wine bag a touch of holiday magic with a flourish of ribbon flowers.

The high-contrast combination of bright red satin damask and soft white and off-white silk ribbon makes a strong yet elegant statement.

Tussie-Mussies

A *tussie-mussie* is a small bouquet of flowers tied with a bow and wrapped in or displayed on a doily. Flowers have conveyed symbolic meaning for hundreds of years, but they gained special significance during the Victorian age, when they became an important means of social communication. Tussie-mussies were given as gifts to express love, praise, admiration, and other sentiments. Creating a tussie-mussie is a unique way to declare your feelings for a friend or loved one. You can make a bouquet that comprises your or your friend's favorite flowers or colors, or you can research the meanings of various flowers in order to communicate a special message. You can also use tussie-mussies as table decorations or party favors (see page 108). As Geraldine Adamich Laufer explains in *Tussie-Mussies* (New York: Workman Publishing Company, 1993), flower symbology can be quite complex—colors as well as flowers have significance—so for simplicity's sake I've provided condensed meanings for the designs that are shown in this book:

- *Peonies* express welcome or wealth

- *Roses* signify love, congratulations, and beauty; *cabbage roses,* which are similar in appearance to roses made with wire-edge ribbon, are "ambassadors of love"

- *Hollyhocks* suggest fertility

- *Chrysanthemums* declare cheerfulness, long life, and joy

- *Pansies* proclaim loving thoughts

- *Poppies* imply forgetfulness or pleasure

- *Daisies* bespeak innocence and simplicity

1. Make the flowers and leaves for your tussie-mussie. Stem them on short, lightweight stems no more than 6 inches long.

2. There are two ways to display flowers in a tussie-mussie. To make the doily cone shown at right, roll a small paper or fabric doily into a cone shape and glue or stitch it in place at the seam. Deposit some glue in the cone, insert the flowers and arrange them as desired, then lightly tie a ribbon bow around the cone. You can also make an arrangement, tie it in place with a bow, then poke the stems through the doily and wrap them together at the back with ribbon or lightweight wire.

SKILL LEVEL

Intermediate

TIME REQUIRED

1½ hours

SUPPLIES

For the flowers, leaves, and bow: Narrow ribbon (1½ inches wide or narrower) in a variety of colors

For the stems: 20-gauge paper-covered wire, ribbon, and glue gun

Paper, fabric, or crocheted doily

General-purpose needle and thread *Use a milliner's needle for lightweight fabrics such as silk and organdy*

This tussie-mussie of miniature roses proclaims love and good wishes.

*Make an easy tussie-
mussie by poking stems
through a doily.*

*Loving thoughts and joy are
given when this tussie-
mussie is presented to that
special someone.*

Holiday Stockings

Santa Claus fans young and old alike love personalized holiday stockings, which are so easy to embellish that you can make a new set every year.

When making design decisions for this project, consider first and foremost the character, color, and fabric of the stocking. (Many craft stores carry undecorated Christmas stockings; if you have trouble finding them in your area, refer to the source directory on page 110.) All of the stocking's attributes should reflect the personality and color preferences of the person whose name it will bear or whose stocking stuffers it will contain. If a stocking feels "right" to you, then the colors and fabrics of the ribbons should complement and harmonize with it.

Make the flowers and leaves, then lay them out on the stocking, experimenting with a few different configurations to see which works best. (The pronounced cuff that appears at the top of many holiday stockings is a great place for decorations.) When you've hit on the best layout, tack or glue the flowers and leaves in place.

SKILL LEVEL
Beginner

TIME REQUIRED
1 hour

SUPPLIES
An undecorated Christmas stocking
Ribbon in a variety of colors and widths
General-purpose needle and thread *Use a milliner's needle for lightweight fabrics such as silk and organdy*
Glue gun (optional)

This formal stocking, which is made from a floral-print fabric in the classic Christmas colors of green and gold, is embellished with red velvet daisies, a gold wire-edge chrysanthemum, green corduroy velvet leaves, and gold "berry" beads.

A stocking made from burgundy velvet, gold lamé, and white lace and decorated with silk roses in a range of pinks embodies the spirit of a Victorian Christmas.

This casual felt stocking with blanket-stitched seams is decorated with poppies made from lightweight felt cut with pinking shears.

Holiday Ornaments

Transform a humble Styrofoam ball into a lavish holiday ornament with some ribbons and a few castoff embellishments. This project is a tribute to my grandmother, who kept my sisters and me busy for hours decorating Styrofoam balls with sequins, beads, faux pearls, and other shiny objects that she collected and stored in her innumerable muffin tins. Here is my version, which uses ribbons instead of sequins.

All free spirits, take note: There are virtually no rules or procedures for this project. Styrofoam balls are made in a range of sizes; you can choose the largest, as long as you have enough ribbon to cover it completely. To make the ornament shown at right, I wound a red-and-gold novelty ribbon around the entire ball, pinning it securely at the bottom and top. I highlighted its equator with a band of Vitruvian scroll or running dog trim, then embellished the top with miniature red pansies and green folded leaves. At the bottom I attached a tassel of 4- to 6-inch red and green ribbons pulled through a large gold bead with a long pin, and at the top a hanger made from the novelty ribbon. But don't let my success with a traditional red-and-green color scheme limit your imagination. Go wherever your creativity takes you—and enjoy the adventure.

This extravagant yet easy-to-make ornament features several ribbons and trims: A Styrofoam ball is wrapped with Renaissance Ribbons "Galon Rococo Multicouleurs" (ribbon #182, color #204), trimmed with Renaissance Ribbons gold trim, and decorated with pansies, folded leaves, and a tassel made with ⅝-inch-wide Hanah Silk in "hot flash" and "forest shadow."

SKILL LEVEL
Beginner

TIME REQUIRED
45 minutes

SUPPLIES
Styrofoam ball
Ribbons in a variety of colors and widths, including novelty ribbons and decorative twines and cords
Embellishments such as sequins, buttons, beads, and charms
Pins
General-purpose needle and thread

Who says Christmas ornaments can only be red and green?

Wreaths

A wreath hung on your front door can announce an event, herald a season, or express a sentiment; hung in a special place, it can complement—or even complete—a decor. A wreath lets friends and family know that they are entering a creative and happy home.

The prospect of creating a wreath can be somewhat intimidating, especially for beginners, because a successful one requires a variety of elements and the careful consideration of their arrangement. By moving forward a step at a time, you'll be far more likely to enjoy the process as it unfolds and to get the results you want.

1. Think about how you can express the occasion or enhance your decor with the colors and textures of small decorative elements. Gradually collect these items from around the house, or purchase them through mail-order catalogs and from craft stores, always keeping in mind that they will somehow have to be attached—either glued, tied, or stitched—to the wreath. Some examples: fresh, dried, or silk flowers and leaves; dried or fresh fruits, vegetables, herbs, and berries; shells; pinecones; buttons, beads, and charms; and any number of small objects.

2. Choose a wreath frame or "blank." Make sure that the material from which the frame is made is not only appropriate for the occasion or decor, but also harmonizes with the colors and textures of the items you've selected. If you're trying to communicate a casual feeling, use a straw or twig wreath; for a more formal appearance, cover a circular wire frame or a foam base with whatever fabric or other material you desire.

3. Now you're ready to choose your ribbons. As you make your selection, again consider the event or decor, then the colors and textures of the decorative elements you collected. If you think your wreath would benefit from a big bow (or two), look for super-wide wire-edge ribbons.

4. Sit down at your work surface with all of your materials in front of you: objects, frame, and ribbons. Look at your blank wreath, then at your ribbons. Decide on the character and color of the background by asking yourself some questions: Do you want a large wire-edge ribbon wound around the wreath, ending in a beautiful bow, or large flowers strategically placed to fill open spaces? Would you like to distribute the elements around the entire wreath, or confine them to just one side or area?

    Once you've chosen the background, imagine the composition of the next level of decoration—the medium-size and small ribbon flowers and the decorative objects. These can be evenly spaced around the larger flowers or in relation to the bow, or arranged in a less symmetrical layout while still creating a balanced presentation.

5. Now we can progress from the theoretical to the concrete: Pick out the flower and leaf designs, then make them. When your flowers are complete, create the background, then begin attaching first the major, then the minor elements. Repeat this incantation to yourself as you work: *It's okay to change your mind.* Give yourself permission to be an artist. That's one of the wonderful things about the creative process.

A twine wreath decorated with ribbon flowers, leaves, and bows, and a touch of lace.

Biel

The Beribboned Table

Centerpieces

Do you want to create or heighten the joyful mood at your next luncheon or dinner party? Make an exquisite ribbon flower centerpiece.

1. Think about the person or the occasion you are celebrating. What kind of atmosphere and color scheme do you want to establish? Then take a look at your linens and tableware to determine whether they can serve as the basis of a suitable color scheme. Think ahead, too: What kinds of supplementary decorations—not only streamers and balloons but beautiful decorative objects like figurines, boxes, or even teapots—would inspire a centerpiece, or enhance the one you're just beginning to imagine? So that there are no unwanted surprises, it's a good idea to actually set the table, or at least part of it, with the linens and tableware you plan to use before you purchase your ribbons and begin making your arrangement. That way, you'll know exactly which ribbon colors, flower sizes and shapes, and vase or container will work best. Also, if you're considering making coordinating napkin rings (see page 106), placecards (page 107), and streamer bouquets (page 108), you don't want to go overboard and create an extravagant centerpiece that will keep you from realizing a complete decorative program.

2. Put the vase or container on the table wherever you're planning to position it within the setting. Place the ribbons for the flowers, leaves, and stems into and around the vase to make sure the colors coordinate with the linens and tableware. If they don't, replace them with others. Step back from the table to see how tall and wide the centerpiece should be. If it makes you feel more confident, take measurements with a yardstick so that you know about how long the stems should be. If necessary or desired, place filler in the bottom of the vase.

3. Make the stemmed flowers using the ribbons you selected. (Don't make all of the stems exactly the same length or your arrangement will look monotonous.) Place each flower in the vase as you make it. When the vase is about half full, stop and assess the arrangement: Does anything seem to be missing? Do you need more flowers in another color or another height? Do you need a few small blooms to fill in, or are there large gaps that cry out for big, lush flowers? Do your stems need more or fewer leaves? As you make more flowers, you may find that you need to remove some of your earlier efforts. See the full-page photographs on pages 31–59 for some arrangement ideas.

4. When the vase is filled with flowers, step back and assess the situation. Does the centerpiece complement the rest of the table? Do the colors, sizes, and textures seem balanced? If everything clicks, you can put it all away until the day of the party. If you think the setting can use a little more excitement, turn the page for more ribbon ideas.

SKILL LEVEL

Intermediate

TIME REQUIRED

Varies, depending on the complexity of the arrangement

SUPPLIES

Ribbons or fabrics in a variety of colors and textures

18- and 20-gauge paper-covered wire

General-purpose needle and thread
Use a milliner's needle for lightweight fabrics such as silk and organdy

Glue gun

Vase or other container(s)

Filler for the base of the arrangement or bottom of the vase, such as florist moss, small stones, or marbles (optional)

Light up your party with an arrangement of ribbon flowers. I devised this yellow, red, and black color scheme for a man's birthday party using a simple grouping of two black-eyed Susans with polymer clay centers and one classic red poppy. I found the unusual picture frame vase in my local Pottery Barn.

Napkin Rings or Ties

Whether for a casual buffet lunch or a formal sit-down dinner, napkin decorations are a fun way to make your occasion seem more special.

1. Before you choose your ribbons, think about how you want to display the napkins within the place setting—to the left of the forks, on the table at the top of the plate beneath the glasses, or on the plate itself? Also consider how much room you will have on the table during the festivities, because you may not want large, cumbersome decorations taking up valuable space after your guests remove them from their napkins.

2. You can use plain purchased napkin rings in the same color as your napkin for a base, or make ties by braiding three pieces of ribbon together. When making the tie, be sure to leave extra ribbon at the beginning and end to create a tasseled effect. (See "Pansy Pouch," page 88, for more information.)

3. Make a flower or two, then glue them to the ring or tie. Make sure their colors complement the centerpiece's, and that their scale is appropriate for the place setting.

SKILL LEVEL

Beginner

TIME REQUIRED

30 minutes per ring

SUPPLIES

Fabric napkins

Undecorated napkin rings (optional)

Ribbons and/or fabrics in harmonizing colors

General-purpose needle and thread
Use a milliner's needle for lightweight fabrics such as silk and organdy

Glue gun (optional)

I continued the yellow, red, and black theme of my centerpiece in my napkin decorations, which feature pansies made from ribbons in red, black-and-yellow check, and black, red, and yellow plaid, along with a red and yellow tasseled tie.

Picture Frame Placecards

Certainly not every occasion needs placecards, but when the opportunity arises you want to do them right. Your guests will take their placecards home as mementos of the gathering, so make sure they're tasteful. Before you decide that your tabletop must have placecards, remember that the more decorative components, the easier it is for the final effect to seem overdone. If you think that your table design would benefit from placecards but would be sent "over the top" if they were decorated with ribbon flowers, buy little silver- or gold-tone picture frames, or paint small unfinished wooden frames with a harmonizing color of acrylic paint.

1. Before you start gluing and sewing, evaluate all of the project elements right on the tabletop: Is the placecard the right size? Does the color of the paint, ribbon, or fabric work with the established color scheme? If you've purchased narrow-width ribbons in addition to those that you used for the centerpiece or napkin rings, do their colors and/or patterns fit? If your answer to all of these questions is "yes," then you're ready to proceed to the next step.

2. Paint the cardboard frame with acrylic paint and let dry, or cover the frame with ribbon or fabric, gluing it in place with a glue gun.

3. Make a few flowers, then experiment with some layouts. Keep in mind that there will be several placecards on the table, so keep the flowers to a minimum and your layout simple.

4. Write the guest's name on a piece of paper or lightweight cardboard. White is a safe choice, but you can use any color that works with your scheme. If desired, embellish the card with paints, rubber stamps, colored pencils, or any medium you prefer. When you're done, insert the completed card in the frame.

5. Repeat steps 2 through 4 for the remaining placecards.

SKILL LEVEL

Beginner

TIME REQUIRED

15 minutes

SUPPLIES

Small cardboard picture frame

For the picture frame: Paint, ribbon, or fabric that matches the established color scheme

For the flowers: Ribbons and/or fabrics in harmonizing colors

General-purpose needle and thread
Use a milliner's needle for lightweight fabrics such as silk and organdy

Glue gun

I decided to emphasize yellow in the placecards so that their bright, sunny color would contrast with the black napkins. I kept the ribbon flowers to a minimum here because I planned to add streamer bouquets to my table decor.

Streamer Bouquets

This project is only for the most ambitious party givers: By hanging decorations above your table, you're telling your guests to expect nothing less than a marvelous time. As exciting as these decorations are, though, their execution requires some restraint and careful thought. When considering possibilities for your ceiling art, don't let your imagination run away with you or you might be discouraged with the result. Two helpful hints: Keep the items lightweight, and restrict the decorations to a specific area—a small one is enough to get the message across. For one Christmas, I created a simple "Visions of Sugarplums Danced in Their Heads" theme by hanging candy canes and other sugary items over the dining room table. Some other suggestions: wire-edge ribbon bows, holiday ornaments, pieces of mistletoe, confetti-filled balloons, fresh or dried seasonal flowers, and handmade flowers with birds and butterflies.

Yet another idea is to make small bouquets similar to the tussie-mussies shown on page 94. To make the hanging bouquet shown opposite, top, I filled a silver-tone cone-shaped holiday ornament with raffia, then inserted short-stemmed ribbon flowers and bows. Part of the fun of making these bouquets is looking for interesting containers. If you don't have containers handy or can't find the right ones, you can always shape a paper doily into a cone, glue it in place, fill it (if desired) with confetti, florist moss, or raffia, then add the stemmed flowers.

To hang your creations, tie the bouquet container to the end of the fishing line without cutting it from the spool. Stand on a stepladder and hold the line to the ceiling to see how far from the table the bouquet should hang, adjusting the length of the line as needed. When the bouquet is suspended at just the right height, cut the line, then use it as a template for cutting the lines for the other bouquets. (Make sure they hang at slightly different heights to create visual variety.) To hang the bouquet, knot the end of the line, then slip a thumbtack into the knot and tack it to the ceiling. (I use tacks so that I don't leave large holes in the ceiling; tape could also be used depending on the weight of the item, but it's more likely to fall.) Continue hanging bouquets until you've created the festive atmosphere you're after.

Sometimes I hang long lengths of silk or curly craft ribbon around the bouquets to fill in gaps and to emphasize particular colors. If you don't mind giving up the table space, you can cut the ribbon so that it's long enough to coil on the table. Sometimes I hang and cut the ribbon so that it becomes an element of the centerpiece.

When you're done, stand back and admire your work. Does anything need to be added, replaced, or taken away? If not, you're ready to party!

SKILL LEVEL

Beginner

TIME REQUIRED

1 hour

SUPPLIES

Lightweight fishing line

For flowers and streamers: Ribbons in various colors and narrow widths

For bows: Wire-edge ribbon

For the stems: 20-gauge paper-covered wire

General-purpose needle and thread
Use a milliner's needle for lightweight fabrics such as silk and organdy

Cone-shaped holiday ornament, paper doily, OR other small, lightweight container

Raffia OR other filler

Glue gun

Ribbon streamer bouquets provide yet another creative outlet for the party decor.

Invert your streamer bouquets to make extravagant curtain tie-backs.

Source Directory

**DIRECT-MAIL SOURCES FOR RIBBON
AND OTHER FLOWERMAKING SUPPLIES**
The following companies sell their products directly to consumers.

Artemis Exquisite Embellishments
179 High Street
South Portland, Maine 04106
(888) 233-5187
http://www.artemisinc.com/
Direct-mail source for Hanah Silk ribbons, "blanks" for several of the projects shown in this book (hats, totes, gift bags, and holiday stockings), and prepackaged kits for the Pansy Pouch (see page 86) and other projects.

Clay Factory of Escondido
750 North Citracado Parkway #21
Escondido, California 92029
(760) 741-3242
http://www.clayfactoryinc.com/
Direct-mail supplier of polymer clay and related products.

Lacis
3163 Adeline Street
Berkeley, California 94703
(510) 843-7178/FAX (510) 843-5018
http://www.lacis.com/
Direct-mail source for ribbons, lace, embellishments, and other sewing-related items, as well as books on various needlearts.

**MANUFACTURERS AND
WHOLESALE DISTRIBUTORS**
The following companies generally sell their products exclusively to sewing and notions, fabric, needlearts, craft, and hobby retailers. If you can't find a store in your area that carries a particular item, or if you need special assistance, a manufacturer's representative will direct you to the retailer nearest you that carries their products.

Creative Kits
Deborrah Henry
70 Irish Road
Rancho de Taos, New Mexico 87557
(505) 751-0656
Wholesale supplier for prepackaged flowermaking kits featuring Hanah Silk ribbons. Also teaches flowermaking classes and workshops nationwide.

Hanah Silk
5155 Myrtle Avenue
Eureka, California 95503
(707) 442-0886; (888) 321-4262

Midori
3524 West Government Way
Seattle, Washington 98199
(206) 282-3595/FAX (206) 282-3431

Mokuba Ribbons
Distributed in the United States by
MKB Ribbon L.L.C.
E.Z. International
95 Mayhill Street
Saddle Brook, New Jersey 07663
(201) 712-1234
http://www.festivegiftwrap.com/

Offray Ribbon
C. M. Offray & Son, Inc.
Distributed in the United States by
Lion Ribbon Company, Inc.
360 Route 24, Box 601
Chester, New Jersey 07930
(908) 8789-4700
http://www.offray.com/

Renaissance Ribbons
13415 Rue Montaigne
P.O. Box 699
Oregon House, California 95962
(916) 692-0842
http://www.rribbons.com/

OF GENERAL INTEREST

Aleene's Creative Living
(800) 686-6014
http://www.aleenes.com/
Several of the flower designs in this book have also been demonstrated on this show, which is broadcast nationwide on The Nashville Network (TNN). Consult your local listings, call the 800 number, or check the Web site for scheduled air dates.

Index

Accessories *(projects)*, 78, 79, 85–89

Bags, gift *(projects)*, 69, 92, 93
Basket
   gift, 92
   storage, 19
Basket of flowers tote *(project)*, 85
Basting, 23
Beribboned table *(projects)*, 102–109
Bias, fabric cut on, 12
Black-eyed Susans
   in centerpiece *(project)*, 104, 105
   design for, 58
"Blooming" hat *(projects)*, 83–84
Bouquet pins *(projects)*, 16
Bouquets
   corsage *(project)*, 81–82
   streamer *(project)*, 108–109
Box, storage, 19
Buttons, for flower centers, 65

Cabbage roses, 94
Centerpieces *(project)*, 102–103
Centers, flower, 53, 64–69
Chrysanthemums
   in corsages, 81
   design for, 46–49
   on holiday stockings *(project)*, 96
   leaves for, 77
   symbology of, 94
Clay, polymer, 69, 104, 105
Color, 14–16, 17, 23, 25, 27, 69, 81, 100
Color temperature, 15
Color wheel, 14, 15, 25
Complementary colors, 14–15, 27
Contrast, 14–15, 16, 25, 26, 27, 69
Cool colors, 15
Copying, 24
Corsages *(projects)*, 80–82
Creative Kits, 9, 86
Creativity, 9, 24–27
Curtain tie-backs *(project)*, 109

Dahlias, design for, 58
Daisies
   centers for, 64, 65
   in corsages *(project)*, 81, 82
   design for, 58–61
   on gift bag *(project)*, 69
   on holiday stockings *(project)*, 96
   symbology of, 94
Dark-to-light arrangement, 24
Designs, flower, 28–61
Doilies, 94–95

Easy leaves, 72
Edges, ribbon, 16
Energy, creative, 25, 27

Fan-folded leaf, 75, 81
Finishing, of flowers, 62–77
Flowers. *See also* specific flower names
   centers of, 64–69
   in corsages *(projects)*, 80–82
   designs of, 28–61
   finishing of, 62–77
   making of, 20–27
   supplies for, 10–19
Folded leaves, 73–75, 80, 81, 98
French knot, 53, 66
French ribbon, 13

Gift bags and baskets, 92, 93
Gifts *(projects)*, 90–97
Gift tie-ons *(projects)*, 92–93
Glue gun/glue sticks, 18, 19

Hanah Silk, 9, 86
Harmony, 14, 15, 16, 26, 27
Hats, "blooming" *(projects)*, 83–84
Holiday ornaments *(projects)*, 98–99
Holiday stockings *(projects)*, 96–97
Hollyhocks
   in corsages *(projects)*, 81, 82
   design for, 42–45
   stems for, 70
   symbology of, 94
   texture of, 16

Internet, 14, 16

Laufer, Geraldine Adamich (author of *Tussie-Mussies*), 94
Leaves
   and creativity, 27
   designs for, 72–77
   easy, 72
   folded, 73–75, 80, 81, 98
   on holiday ornaments *(project)*, 98
   on holiday stockings *(projects)*, 96
   scalloped, 76, 82, 84
   texture of, 16
   wired, 77
   and wire-edge ribbon, 13
   in wreaths *(project)*, 100, 101

Mini-tassel, 68

Napkins rings or ties *(project)*, 106
Needles, 18, 19

On the bias, cutting fabric, 12
Organdy ribbon, 12
Originality, 24
Ornaments, holiday *(project)*, 98–99

Pansies
   centers for, 64, 66, 67
   colors, textures, and ribbon width for, 17
   design for, 50–53
   as gift tie-ons *(project)*, 93
   on hats *(project)*, 83, 84
   on holiday ornaments *(project)*, 98
   on napkin ties *(project)*, 106
   on placecards *(project)*, 107
   on pouch *(project)*, 86–89
   in streamer bouquets *(project)*, 109
   symbology of, 94
   in tussie mussies *(projects)*, 95
Peonies
   design for, 34–37

Peonies (continued)
  ribbon width for, 17
  symbology of, 94
  texture of, 16
  and wire-edge ribbon, 13
  without basting, 23
Picots, 16
Pins, bouquet *(projects)*, 16
Placecards, picture frame
  (project), 107
Pleated ribbon, 12, 16
Polyester ribbon, 12
Polymer clay, 69, 104, 105
Poppies
  in centerpieces *(project)*, 104,
  105
  centers for, 64
  design for, 54–57
  on holiday stockings *(project)*,
  97
  leaves for, 72
  symbology of, 94
  and wire-edge ribbon, 13
Posies, design for, 30–33
Pouch, pansy *(project)*, 86–89
Preparation, ribbon, 22
Pressing
  of flowers, 27
  of ribbons, 22
Primary colors, 14, 15

Ribbon flowers. *See* Flowers;
  specific flower names
Ribbons, 12–13
  for centers, 66
  preparation of, 22
  shopping for, 14–17
  soft-edge, 12
  wire-edge, 13

Rinsing, of ribbons, 22
Roses
  in corsages *(projects)*, 80–82
  design for, 38–41
  as gift tie-ons *(projects)*, 92, 93
  on hats *(project)*, 84
  on holiday stockings *(project)*,
  97
  leaves for, 75, 76
  stems for, 70, 95
  symbology of, 94
  texture of, 16
  in tussie-mussies *(projects)*, 94,
  95
  value in, 16
  and wire-edge ribbon, 13
  without basting, 23

Satin ribbon, 16
Scalloped leaves, 76, 82, 84
Scissors, 18, 19
Secondary colors, 14, 15
Selvedges, 12
Shade, 15, 27
Shopping, for ribbons, 14–17
Silk ribbon, 12, 13
Size, of flower
  and layout, 27
  ribbon width and, 17
Soft-edge ribbon, 12
Special occasions *(projects)*,
  90–101
Squiggly, 67
Stems
  in centerpieces *(project)*, 104
  design for, 70–71
  easy leaves onto, 72
  in tussie-mussies *(project)*, 95
  for variety, 27

Stockings, holiday *(projects)*,
  96–97
Storage box/basket, 19, 27
Streamer bouquets *(project)*,
  108–109
Suede ribbon, 12
Supplies, 10–19

Table, beribboned *(projects)*,
  102–109
Tassels
  on holiday ornaments *(project)*,
  98, 99
  mini-, 68
Temperature, color, 15
Texture, 16, 17, 23, 27, 69, 81,
  100
Thimbles, 18
Thread, 18, 19
Tie-backs, curtain *(project)*, 109
Tie-ons, gift *(projects)*, 92–93
Tint, 15, 27
Tone, 15, 27
Tote, basket of flowers *(project)*,
  85
Tussie-mussies *(projects)*, 94–95

Value, 15, 16, 25
Variegated ribbon, 12, 13, 16
Velvet ribbon, 12, 27, 83

Warm colors, 15
Wearables *(projects)*, 27, 78–84
Width, ribbon, 17, 23
Wired leaves, 77
Wire-edge ribbon, 13
  and basting, 23
Wire/wire cutters, 18, 19
Wreaths *(project)*, 100–101